PLAYWRIGHT AT WORK

Douglas Ebersole

John van Druten.

PLAYWRIGHT AT WORK

John van Druten

GREENWOOD PRESS, PUBLISHERS
WESTPORT, CONNECTICUT

To

CARTER

Who Said:

"Write It All Down"

CONTENTS

PLAYWRIGHT AT WORK

CHAPTER ONE

What This Book Is

I HAVE been a playwright for more than twenty-five years. It was almost the only thing I ever wanted to be. It is still the thing that a great many people want to be. And if they do not, it is something that they want to hear about; they come and ask me questions; they come and listen and ask more questions when I have been invited to lecture on the trade of playwriting. It is because of them that I am trying to write this book.

In doing so, as in writing a play, I should know, and perhaps state, just what I am aiming at. This is not to be a book of rules. I am by no means sure that such a thing is a possibility. I know that in America, where I live now as a citizen, there are a great many college courses in playwriting, and remembering the list of playwrights who attended those of Professor George Pierce Baker at Harvard and at Yale, I realize that those courses do some good, although I wonder whether those same playwrights would not have happened anyway. In England, where I was

1

brought up, there were no such courses. In a prejudiced way, it would have been assumed that playwriting was not a thing that could be taught; perhaps, even, that it was not a thing that ought to be taught. It was an accidental, and only occasionally profitable, gift that happened to one. But even if I still slightly share the English point of view, I know that when the desire and the will to become a playwright are there, there are things that can be learned, if only to help shorten the days of one's apprenticeship. In my own days of playwriting, I have learned a lot of these things. Perhaps some of them are no longer true or valuable. I cannot be sure of that. I, too, like all other playwrights, can become old-fashioned overnight.

That is a great dread with playwrights. It seems to happen to them more quickly than to any other kind of artist—the moment when they must say, as Sir Arthur Pinero and Henry Arthur Jones, both playwrights of the first importance just before and during my early youth, said: "They don't want me any more." One can awake to that fact with the fall, or even the rise, of a curtain any day. One can awake to it with the reception of one's latest script by the manager to whom it has been submitted. The play is out of date, the theater has passed one by, the rules with which one grew up are no longer of value. It seems wiser, therefore, when I have not long ago produced a successful play in New York, to assume that it has not yet happened to me, and that some of the things that I know and believe about playwriting are still true and useful, and that this is a moment when it is still safe to try to set them down for others to read. That is the purpose of this book. It is written in 1952, after the production of a play called *I Am a Camera*, based on Christopher Isherwood's short stories.

That play was the result of twenty-five years and more of playwriting. There were things in it which I would not have done before, and things which I would not have known how to do, because no one else had done or even sketched them to show me that they were possible or desirable; the years had indicated that they might be. It makes, as a play, a number of mistakes, which do not seem to have hurt it too badly. It breaks some rules because I wanted to do so, and others because I either did not know of them or else could not avoid their breakage. I do not think it a perfect play; I am by no means sure that it is my best play (and I do not think one should consider things like that, anyway); but it was the best that I could write last year on the given subject matter. The contents of this book will be some of the things that I knew, things I have read, been told, have picked up, thought of for myself, in the years that I have practiced the job.

I have always read a great deal about playwriting. I have read a great deal of dramatic criticism, and I would advise all playwrights to do the same. I think that they should read every word of Bernard Shaw's *Dramatic Opinions,* and of Max Beerbohm's *Around Theatres.* The fact that the majority of plays covered in those volumes will be plays they have never heard of, and maybe would not even be able to get hold of if they tried, does not matter. Reading the words of those two masters (and they still are that to me) will teach them a great deal about the theater, and will maintain their excitement over it. They will retain or reject what they need to, but the substratum of theater knowledge and wisdom will be thickened by their reading. I think they should also read a good deal of George Jean Nathan, though he will disillusion them more than a little. And they should read plays, almost any plays. Something will be learned from each.

Books on playwriting, books as to how it is done, I would be more chary of advising. These books have always depressed me, convinced me that I know little or nothing about the job. The rules frighten me, because I can never be sure whether I have kept to them. They make me feel like the centipede, when it was asked which leg went after which. That, you may remember, raised its mind to such a pitch, it lay distracted in a ditch, considering how to run. An interviewer the other day asked me if I always followed the old rule that the first act of a play should be the noun, the second act the verb, and the third act the predicate in the sentence which was the play. I had never heard of the rule, but I immediately began to wonder if it were true, if it ought to be true, if I had obeyed it, if I ought to obey it.

It reminded me of another rule I had once heard, in which some famous playwright had said: "First, I tell them what I am going to do, then I do it, then I tell them I have done it." I had long pondered this and had decided that it really made a play one act only, the second act in which the author was doing his job, and that I thought there should be more to the task than that, but it had worried me for a long time as to whether the plays that I was trying to write followed it closely enough.

The same thing was true when I became a director. I was very frightened at the prospect of my first production. I went to two men for advice. One was a young director whom I admired. He pulled a large sheet of paper toward him, and proceeded to draw a stage. Then he divided up this stage into sections, and showed me which section was the most important. (It was Front Stage Right—the place, he assured me, where newspapers printed the sharpest morning news, and therefore the place to play one's most important action.) He drew a lot of arrows, talked about zones and levels, and left me even more frightened than I had been.

The other man to whom I went was Joshua Logan, who had stage-managed an earlier play of mine and had since started his career as one of the best stage directors. I asked him about my problem. His answer was a very simple and a very heartening one. "All you have to do," he said, "is to use your common sense, and see that the play looks well. You have watched your plays directed for years by a very fine director, and you have perfectly good taste of your own. And don't ever be afraid of telling your actors that you don't know something. You don't have to be infallible to keep their respect."

That was wonderful. It heartened me completely. I feel very much the same about the rules of playwriting. Use your common sense. But there were other important words in Logan's advice. "You have watched your plays directed for years by a very fine director." That director was Auriol Lee, and I had learned by watching her, by listening to her, by picking things up from her. She was a woman who knew her job. My feeling about this book is that it may operate in something of the same way. I like to think of myself as a man who knows his job, or who knows something about it. I know my own practice of it, my virtues and my faults. Perhaps from me a few things can come which may be of help to others interested in the same profession—the profession of playwriting. I am not teaching. I suppose the old rule is still true, that he who can does, and he who cannot teaches. But I am trying to help. That, at least.

It was just as I was about to start this book that I came upon a sentence in an essay by Clifford Bax. "Plays," he said, "are a 'perishable commodity,' because with a few magnificent exceptions, they succeed only if, like journalism, they express the outlook and appeal to the interests of a fleeting phase in social life. Most readers prefer the newspaper to a literary classic, and most playgoers visit a theatre not in the hope of seeing a beautiful work of art, but of hearing a commentary upon the grim or comic aspects of everyday life."

This passage stopped me for a moment. It seemed an odd remark, coming from as skilled and sensitive a playwright as Clifford Bax has been (I think he is little known here, but his reputation in England, though slender, is a gracious one). I remembered the long passages in Somerset Maugham's book *The Summing Up,* in which he explained his reasons for leaving the theater, and I turned back to them. They were, by and large, the same reasons, more forcefully, more trenchantly put. "Ephemeral" is the word he uses for the theater, though he covers himself by excepting plays written in verse. Perhaps that is what Clifford Bax means by his "few magnificent exceptions." Plays in verse are not ephemeral, not perishable commodities; plays in prose seem to be. That, very briefly, was why Maugham left the theater.

I had very slightly resisted Maugham when I first read his book, thinking that his wording was a little too obviously urbane, cynical and indifferent, coming from a man who had so well and so skillfully practiced a theatrical gift. It seemed to me that there was a touch too much contempt in his appraisal of it. Clifford Bax, too, I thought perhaps a shade self-deprecatory. Yet, in many ways, I agree with them. The theater is ephemeral, and plays are a perishable commodity. But so, I thought, are a great many things. The average novel is almost more so, when one looks at the fiction shelves of any secondhand bookstore. A good deal of music is. Who now remembers Spohr as a composer, though his name occurs, joined with those of Bach and Beethoven, in the Gilbert and Sullivan aria: "A More Humane Mikado"? The art of all interpretive performers is completely ephemeral, dying with the artist, be he or she ever so great. I have seen Karsavina dance, and have heard Yvette Guilbert sing. I can imagine no artistry greater than theirs, but I cannot describe it to you, and if I could, it would be my description rather than their art which would remain with you. The art of cookery, of the manufacture of perfumes, of growing flowers, of anything designed to please the human tastes, these too are perishable and ephemeral. But it does not mean that, within their limitations, they are trivial, unimportant or not worth pursuing.

As to the exception of plays in verse from the ephemeral standard, I am inclined to doubt the validity of that. There is a kind of snobbishness about poetry, although Clifford Bax, being a poet himself, should not share in it. One can excuse a great deal by murmuring: "It's poetry," if anyone attacks it. People are ashamed not to like poetry, if they have been told that it is good. But apart from Shakespeare (everything is always apart from Shakespeare), how many verse plays have remained better than their prose brothers, in English, at any rate? A couple of Marlowe's, perhaps of Webster's; Shelley's *The Cenci,* maybe, just maybe; none of Browning or of Tennyson. I can still remember how popular was the poet-dramatist, Stephen Phillips, in the earlier years of this century. Clifford Bax, in the same book, lists a selection of the things the better critics said of him. Who, under my own age, has heard of him now? The same things are being said of Christopher Fry and of T. S. Eliot today. They have been said of Maxwell Anderson. One wonders. Dead poetry can be almost deader than dead prose, even if its form is dramatic.

If the theater is perishable and ephemeral, I see no reason for being ashamed of one's part in it, nor for avoiding the effort to do one's best at it. To resign from it for that reason would suggest that one has substituted something of greater and more permanent significance. I would find it hard to know what can definitely be said to be. I am still happy to be writing plays; I shall be happier if I can write better plays, and I shall not think of them as journalism. I shall be happy if more and more people can write better plays, and more and more better plays. When I was small, I used to read Samuel French's catalogue of plays with admiration and envy. It contained a list of playwrights with ten or twenty plays under their names. That is what I want to see. I do not think a man is a fully developed playwright without them.

I cannot make you into a playwright. I cannot make you a successful playwright. How could I, with a longish record that is almost fifty-fifty in its successes and failures behind me? All that I can do is to add anything I know from my own experience that may help you in your playwriting. I can tell you only what I know and think, myself. There will be no rule that is not covered with the phrase "to suit my tastes." Those tastes may very well not be yours, as they have often not been those of other people, sometimes of the majority of other people. But they are all that I can write. They are going to be what I will tell you, as well as how I, myself, set about the job, what are the problems and conditions that I have to meet, and the best ways that I know in which to handle them.

CHAPTER TWO

My Own Beginnings, and Yours

I MUST, therefore, start with myself. I must, in fact, remain a great deal with myself. A large number of my illustrations, for bad as well as for good, must come from my own works. There is no conceit in that. My own plays are the ones that I know best, and I know why I did or did not do certain things in them. Also, I think it would be ungracious in one playwright to belittle others in his profession. What examples I use from other playwrights—from other living playwrights, anyway—will be almost entirely the things that seem to me to be good in their works. I shall omit much, I am aware, and I shall always regret the good things that I might have stated.

Quite a few of the illustrations that I use from others will be from old plays, plays that the younger of my readers may not know. There are reasons for that. Among them is the fact that they are plays which I studied when I was younger, and which contain things that seem of value still to me. Most of them are theater classics, of one kind or another. I have several times used *The Second Mrs. Tanqueray*, by Sir Arthur Pinero. This, in its own time, was a daring play; it was thought a very modern play; and it also managed a highly useful trick, which was to make its audiences think that they were getting something highbrow, advanced and intellectual, and at the same time to offer them a highly enjoyable entertainment. If you can do that, you have really won the game hands down—for the moment, at any rate. Time may show things differently, as it has done with *Mrs. Tanqueray*. There was nothing seriously intellectual in that play, and it had borrowed almost not at all from Ibsen, as so many people thought that it had. It survived because it was good entertainment. I would recommend every student of playwriting to read it. And where I need to, I feel that I can attack it without presumption, now.

This will apply to other old plays. Remember, too, that those were the plays that, because I grew up with them, had a quality of magic for me, a magic which still remains. It is a magic that has often little to do with the play itself; it is the magic of one's own first encounter with what the play contained. I am always chary of going to revivals of anything that I once liked. I can never be sure whether the failure to recapture the early enchantment is due to the play itself, or to the performance. I have reread novels which seemed to me powerful and important when I was in my twenties, and have found them a great deal weakened, and that what looked like solid scenery is now only made of obvious *papier-mâché*. I know that these are not the great novels, and that ones like *Anna Karenina* and *War and Peace* will not weaken, but they were the good novels of my youth, they communicated a magic to me. And if a great deal of that magic was in myself, I would rather keep it there, in my own memory. The plays that you may read because I shall mention them may not have it for you. Then you will miss nothing. Perhaps you will be able to see why they may once have had it for others, or they may be completely empty for you now. Even that fact may be of some help to you.

I have spoken of twenty-five years of playwriting as my own experience. I should, actually, have made it a larger figure. It should have gone back to the time when I could first put a pencil to paper. I always wanted to write plays. How or why that happens, I do not know. It happens to all sorts of people, even to those who, because of where they were brought up, have never seen a play performed. I am under the impression that I started my own first play before I had ever seen one acted. How did I know about the dramatic form? How do any of those people know of it? I do not know the answer. I know only that anything written in dialogue has always had an instantaneous appeal to me, so long as it reflected—or seemed to do—the quality of real speech. Even now, I am still fascinated by the advertisements, the scraps of conversation heard on the radio, where husbands and wives, mothers and neighbors, explain, in terms of their own life, why they use this or that commercial product. The ear, the ear that assimilates the tones and idioms of speech, that can pick out and dramatize a way of living, a set of domestic circumstances, from a conversation, is the first qualification of the playwright, as the eye is the first for a painter. A gift for reproduction, a power of selection, are what he needs most to develop.

I began my playwriting with historical plays. The first that I can remember was about Anne Boleyn. I did not write very much of it. I did not create any of it. I can remember describing the setting, with Anne seated in her bower, and Henry the Eighth appearing. I could not think what they could talk about. I asked my brother, who was eight years older. (I was not more than seven, myself.) He suggested that the King might ask her if she preferred living in the country to the town. That seemed to me a fine opening. I wrote it. Three lines of it. Then I gave up again. I could think of nothing else for them to say. My brother finished the play for me. I can remember only one line from it. It came from Henry, addressing Cardinal Wolsey. "Thou bungling fool," he cried. "And for this have I made thee my Chancellor!" I thought that wonderful, then; I still do not think it too bad. It seems to me to have both character and comedy in it.

From *Anne Boleyn* I went to *Mary, Queen of Scots,* and actually finished a play about her, all by myself. It took, I think, three pages of foolscap, and I can remember only one thing about it. That was a stage direction, for which my mother teased me. It will recur when I reach the question of stage directions later on. After that, my playwriting stopped for a long time, as far as actual penmanship went. But I had a toy stage, and was given to performing plays on it, with figures cut from fashion books as the characters. These plays were almost all based on what I had heard of current popular successes. A scrap of dialogue, a description of one moment in a play, a picture in a magazine, and I was off to try to reproduce it, to elaborate on it, to make a play from it. I listened to everything I could hear of the current theater. I read all the casts in the papers, what I could find of dramatic criticism, studied all the photographs and the programs. I absorbed the theater through every open pore. Mine was not a theatrical family, and no one from the theater ever entered our house. But my parents were fond of it; they both had had continental educations, and they considered the theater a part of good and intelligent living. It was important to them, and they did not mind—at that time, at any rate—my own preoccupation with it. They fed it well for me.

When I was about fourteen, I started to write plays again. I began with one-act plays. Too many people do. It seems to be regarded as an easier start on the professional journey. I would not think of it as such. The one-act play seems to me quite extraordinarily difficult of achievement, needing enormous compression, and a high degree of technical facility. I greatly doubt if I could write such a thing, myself, now, but in those days I tried to write a great many. They were bad, very bad. There were two or three that were written about domestic servants, with the action placed in the kitchen. I assume that this was because, at that time, I knew, as do so many English children, the servants better than I knew my own family, spending a great deal of my time with them. That reason seems to me a good one still. One must write what one knows best. I also found the talk of servants a good chance for jokes, based largely on mispronunciations and malapropisms. That aspect of playwriting, I now consider a bad one, a very bad one.

Again, when I was about seventeen, playwriting left me. I switched to short stories, and to poetry, and neither of these did me much good. At last, soon after I was twenty, I returned to the theater, and I stayed there. I wrote my first full-length play, and that broke a fear for me, the fear of writing a second and a third act. It seemed a job of so vast a length that I did not think that I could last it out. A friend who was staying with me told me—almost as a kind of bet or dare—to sit down and begin. "You know what the play is to be about. You know your characters. You know roughly what the act divisions are to be. Sit down now," he bade me, "and start to write. Stay here in your own room for at least three hours, and write. See what happens." I obeyed him. I wrote a great deal in the next three hours; presently, I finished the play. Later, it very nearly got performed at a theater in Dublin. At least, the parts were actually typed. I had started.

I still have the script of that play. I have just reread it for the first time in very many years. There is a great deal to be learned from it, good and bad. It illustrates a number of things that are true of all young playwrights. Bits of it have pleased me to re-read, and a good deal of it has shocked me. I know, I think, exactly why the good and the bad things were there, and why they were as they were. For the sake of the things that I can show from it, I would like to tell its plot, and a little of its history. They will both serve a good many purposes.

The play takes place in a London suburban house that was very like my own home, and the home of the friend who urged me to write the play. The hero is a young man of just over twenty-one, which is what I must have been at the time. He has been away with his parents for a Christmas holiday to a sea-side hotel, and has had an affair with a young married woman whom he met there. The affair has gone on, since. The first twenty minutes of the play are taken up with establishing the home and the relationships of the family. They are not badly done. I knew what I was writing about, and I was getting a great deal out of my system: a great deal of boredom and resistance. The mother is weakly sketched, and there is a portrait of an objectionable aunt which, considering that I was drawing it from a real one, seems to me quite extraordinary in its feebleness and inadequacy. I cannot think why I did not really let myself go there. But the father is well drawn, and there is also a sister, taken almost entirely from the sister of my friend, who is well conceived. She is real and warm and honest and sincere, and she has some wit and some sparkle about her. I was given to writing that character quite often in those days—the truthful, forthright girl of urgent common sense and wisdom, expressing herself forcibly and pungently.

In the middle of the first act (when the other characters have been removed by some of the feeblest technical devices I have ever read) the hotel woman is announced. The sister is on the stage then, and her brother merely asks her to leave, which she does. This I still consider an admirable touch. It saves any trouble of working up an excuse for an exit, and it gives a good picture of the intimacy of the brother-and-sister relationship. Then the play goes bad for quite a long time. The woman is going to have a baby, and she has come to tell that fact. The telephone was carefully put out of order on page one. The scene between the two of them is quite dreadful. Such a situation had never happened to me or to anyone I had met, and I did not know anyone like the woman. I was merely guessing, and writing for theatrical effect. The dialogue is, in almost every word, hysterical, false and unbelievable.

In Act Two, the woman's husband has started divorce proceedings. Almost the whole act is taken up with the boy breaking the news to his family, and with their reception of it. It is well written. The father's initial reaction is broader and more conventional than I now like, but I am not sure yet that it would not have been that of my own father. The boy, himself, is on the whining and somewhat hysterical side, but there are some good moments even in his behavior, and a few very natural touches in the whole act, when some flash of real inspiration, of true absorption in my characters, overtook my inept theatrical sense. The boy's attitude is that he must marry the woman, even though he despises her. The prospect of the child, the thought of a son of his own, is more important to him than anything else. He is to be a father, a father at twenty-one, and that comes first.

His own parents share his attitude after the first shock has evaporated. His sister does not. She has a long and highly impassioned speech, making a good deal of sense, over the sentimental nonsense they are all talking. The act ends with the birth of a new kind of understanding '(which a stage direction rather oddly describes as "spiritual") between father and son, and the rebreaking of it by the boy's bitterness.

The last act is awful, so bad that I dread describing it. The woman is living in the house with them now. She has a drunken cockney maid, who is everything that I most dislike in playwriting. She and the maid have a row, and the maid, in revenge, tells the hero that he was not the only man in her mistress' life. There was another, a Frenchman, whose child the forthcoming baby may just as easily be. From there I go on to one of the most determinedly unhappy endings a young playwright ever forced himself to. The hero has decided to reject her, but she torments him with the picture of what doing so will be like for him, the pity and sympathy he will have to endure from his family, and all the "I Told You So's" that he will have to hear. That is too much for him, and he decides to say nothing, but to marry her all the same. This I now flatly refuse to believe. I know why I wrote it. I know there was a situation where a good friend of mine went ahead with a marriage he disbelieved in because he thought his family was on the girl's side, and he lacked the courage to face them and her with his own changed mind. But that was not what I was writing here. I was youthfully determined to write something powerfully artistic and unhappy, and it is, quite frankly, absolute nonsense.

The play seems to me now to be compounded of flaws and virtues. That is why I have spent so long on it, and why I want to spend a little longer. Its main virtue, as I now see it, is that it was about something, and for the most part something I knew well. It lacks many of the tricks and devices that I had previously thought must be put into plays to make them attractive. I had been told by a girl-friend that it was a good idea to give my characters jolly nicknames to brighten the play, and had in an earlier play invented a man named Lionel Samuel Drury, for no other purpose than he could be called L. S. D. (pounds, shillings and pence) by the other characters, and further jokes about money were continually being made around him. I dropped this kind of thing in the present play. I was not writing from the memory of other plays, and I was dressing things up very little. I was writing as truthfully and sincerely as I knew how.

Also, I was saying something that was important to me. I was, myself, in a slight state of protest against my home, and more so against my friend's home, and I was voicing the eternal rebellion of the younger generation against its elders. I was interested in the father-and-son relationship, the two who had never really understood each other, but were brought to sympathy and a reciprocal emotion by a situation in the play, even though here I threw it away again. The main thesis, the young man caught by his own diversion of adultery, has truth to it, and his attitude toward parenthood, though slightly exaggerated, is not a wholly untruthful one. All of these things I could write because I knew them, because they were true for me, and I was writing from my own sincere feelings.

Where the play went hopelessly wrong was when I began to write of things I did not know, and where I tried to interject the element of plot. The woman does not exist, even as a bad-tempered and hysterical bitch, which is all that is shown of her. There is no vestige of anything attractive about her, and no stage directions saying that she was pretty are going to make any difference. I have no idea why or how she came to be staying at that seaside hotel at Christmas all by herself. I do not know how she lived, except that she had a flat close by, a fact which seemed to the mother to make things worse. This I still think to be a good touch. Otherwise, the woman is merely the recipient of an affair, and her reaction to the news that she is going to have a baby is that of a small girl of twelve. There is no touch of worldliness, of sophistication, of polish or even of skillful cunning in her, and one of these things was needed. The existence of the Frenchman, or of any other men in her life, is not suggested until I needed it quite suddenly for my last-act plot. It is neither true nor false of her to say that there were other men in her life, because there is neither truth nor falsity in her. I had no ideas about her at all, and little faith in her situation.

But at least, there was a play there, and I had learned a great deal about playwriting. The charge against the woman as an unreal character came back to me from almost everyone who read the manuscript. I would not believe them then, but in the end they won out on me, and I came, too, to meet people who were a little more like what she should have been, and I learned from them how I should have written her. I still had to learn not to try to write what I did not know, but in the play I was creating from a basis that was at least fifty per cent familiar, true and valid for me, and that was a great deal. It brings me to what I want to say next, as the first and most important thing about playwriting.

If any would-be author were to come to me and say that he wanted to write a play, asking my advice on it, my first question would be: "Do you want to write *a* play, or is there an especial play that you want to write?" If the answer were that he wanted to write *a* play, just any play so long as it was a play, then I would start to worry, and I would try to worry him. It is a dangerous frame of mind. It means, merely, that the theater, just as such, has attracted him for some reason (and there are a number of bad reasons), and that he is loose in its formless limbo. That is how bad plays get written; plays with no purpose or objective at all; just plays, if that. It is a state of mind that besets us all, even the experienced writers. When we have written nothing for a long time, the urge to get to work again can be overpowering. There is the dread that we have dried up, and will never write again. We grasp at anything, write almost anything, because at least we are writing. This would not matter if one were prepared to do it merely as an exercise, determined to throw the whole thing, afterward, into the wastebasket. But one never is; that sacrifice is something no author can be asked to make. The wisest thing to do is to try to resist the impulse, to forget it. The next best thing is to attempt an adaptation, using whatever skill one may have learned upon someone else's work. And even there, it is wiser that the book one is adapting should make its own especial appeal, have for the adaptor some significance that he seriously wants to see on a stage.

It is not wise to go around hunting for a theme or a plot. "Alfred is searching for a theme," wrote Mrs. Tennyson to a friend. I well understand Alfred's plight, but that was not the best solution for it. The themes that arrive when one is seeking for them are liable to be false ones, of one's own devising. The only theme worth having is the one that comes and insists on being written.

I realize that that can sound like an affected thing to say, and that themes do not really come and insist on anything. But since the whole business of writing is a totally mysterious thing, springing from one knows not what source, and since the best things that one writes seem to arrive as total surprises even to the author, who is apt to stop and say: "Now, how did I know that?"—since the whole impulse comes from some uncomprehended spring of one's being, some other level of consciousness, some compulsion that one does not understand, there is a good deal more truth to it than may at first seem likely. The wisest thing to do to a theme once it occurs is to try and forget it. Try not to play with it. Try to leave it alone, and see if it comes haunting you, if you awake with it still uppermost in your mind in the morning, if bits and pieces have added themselves to it without your having—apparently—done anything to achieve them. Presently, if that has happened, you will not be able to stop yourself from going to the typewriter. Then you are on your way. But try to be sure, first.

There is a poem of Robert Graves that seems to me to exemplify this. It is called "A Pinch of Salt." It runs as follows:

> When a dream is born in you
>   With a sudden clamorous pain,
> When you know the dream is true
>   And lovely, with no flaw nor stain,
> O then, be careful, or with sudden clutch
> You'll hurt the delicate thing you prize so much.
>
> Dreams are like a bird that mocks,
>   Flirting the feathers of his tail.
> When you seize at the salt-box,
>   Over the hedge you'll see him sail.
> Old birds are neither caught with salt nor chaff:
> They watch you from the apple bough and laugh.
>
> Poet, never chase your dream.
>   Laugh, yourself, and turn away.
> Mask your hunger, let it seem
>   Small matter if he come or stay.
> But when he nestles in your hand at last,
> Close up your fingers tight and hold him fast.

I notice on the copy of *Fairies and Fusiliers,* to which I turned to check my memory of this, the date on the flyleaf in my own handwriting—Christmas, 1919. Had I learned that message by then? I am sure I had not. I suppose one never wholly learns it. The birds are sometimes too tempting, the hand goes out too soon, the salt-box is grabbed at, and the bird flies, leaving, it may be, a few tail feathers behind him. These are all that is left to make the play. "Poet, never chase your dream." It is a hard lesson.

Suppose, however, the author admits that it is not *a* play

that he wants to write, but an especial play, that he knows its story or its theme, and that this is it. I think my next question would be: "Why do you want to write this particular play?" and the more difficulty he finds in answering that question, the better pleased I shall be. Actually, the only real answer is: "Because I want to. Because it excites me." And the answer to that one is: "God bless you. Go ahead." But it is still well to try and be sure why. There are so many answers, so many bad answers. When I was still in my early twenties, I had a plot I wanted to write. It was to be a light comedy. An agent, and a good one, asked me why I wanted to write that plot. I answered that I thought it would "go down well," and I brought on myself one of the severest tirades I have ever heard. "What a perfectly dreadful reason for wanting to write a play—because you think it will go down well. If you have *got* to write it, because the idea fascinates you and you can't leave it alone, then you must write it, however slight or bad it is, but not because you think it would go down well." This was true. I knew it was true. It was all that I had ever been told, from the moment when J. C. Squire, the poet, told me that no artist had ever produced a genuine work of art unless he were first sincerely moved by his subject. I did not wholly believe him then, but I came very soon to do so. I believe him totally now. "It will go down well," is no answer. "Are you moved by the subject—or amused by it—or aren't you?" That is the essential query. And: "Why are you?" is the next one. Is it because of some other play you have seen which this indirectly suggests? Are you trying merely to reproduce an emotion that you received totally from literature? Are you trying to write a part for this or that star? Do you think this is the right moment for a play on this or that political subject?

These are the wrong reasons. You will forget their wrongness, or fail to ask yourself the questions, many times in your life, but the wrongness will be there always.

If, as I have already said, there is no answer, except that the idea does move you, then you have a good chance. All that you have to do then is to try to make sure that it will move your audience in the same way. And that is where construction and technique and the rest of this book come in. There are a few other things I would like to say first. I have often thought it a good thing to ask yourself whether anyone else could write the play as well as you could, or whether there is something in the idea that is especially your own. The family relationships in my own play that I have outlined seem to me to have been my own. There have been many other plays about suburban families, but there were things in this one, aspects in this one, that I think were only mine to know and write. That is what is good about the play. If the writer feels that any other author of talent knows as much about his subject as he himself does, he would be wiser to abandon it. There have been very many plays about retired actresses with two children and a writer husband. It was a favorite formula for young playwrights in the twenties and thirties. But there has been only one really good one, which was Noel Coward's *Hay Fever*. Noel Coward knew a great deal more about that kind of household than anyone else did. He was drawing it very largely from a real one—only a real one could possibly have been so extraordinary—and his knowledge, his amusement, his certainty of what he was doing gave life to the play.

There is another question that is often suggested as a test of a theme's validity: the question of universality. How much will this theme be able to be identified by the audiences as having application to themselves? Without such an identification, we are told, the play is unlikely to be successful. This is a harder question to deal with. Basically, it has a good deal of truth to it. If a young man who had been raised in a Tibetan village came with the idea for a serious play based on the fact that a Tibetan woman is morally expected to share her husband with a number of other women, and that monogamy for women is considered selfish and immoral there, I should worry a little over its acceptance by New York audiences. I would feel that it would be hard to make them sympathize with the ostracism of a girl who wanted to keep her man all to herself, or to make them feel she was an important pioneer in opposing her family, her friends and all society in her wish to do so. The same objection seems to me to apply to a great deal of Greek tragedy. When I saw *Oedipus* not long ago, I could not resist a feeling of deep impatience. I wanted to say: "Oh, do stop bothering yourself so. You couldn't help it, you really couldn't. The circumstances were dead against you. It's unfortunate, but you needn't go on like that about it. Although, since you knew of the curse beforehand, why you wanted to go and marry a woman old enough to be your mother, and not make sure that she wasn't, is something that also alienates my sympathy from you. But you don't have to go and blind yourself, you really don't." I feel slightly the same over *King Lear,* but those are things one is supposed to keep quiet about. And in any case, *Oedipus* and *Lear* have other and greater qualities to recommend them.

But it is true that the play should have a form of universal emotion (the circumstances need not be universal at all) to recommend it. The audience should be able to recognize the situation, participate in its problems, and identify itself with its hero or heroine in some way, even if that identification is based merely on envy, which is how the movies normally achieve it. The luxury, the money, the glamoured fame of the characters (if they can be called that) in movies is what wins the audiences' participation in their problems.

Here, then, are the first questions. Have you an especial play? Why does it appeal to you? Is it, in any way, your own, more especially yours than anyone else's? Will the audiences be able to share your especial emotion about it, and make it their own, too? If the answer to all of these is yes, then you can start thinking about writing it.

CHAPTER THREE

Theme, Story, Plot and Mood

H OW MUCH of your play do you already know? How much can you tell of it? What is its theme, its story, its plot or its mood? I think you had better tell me.

Now this business of telling is an important one. Should one tell anyone about the new play? My answer is, as few people as possible. For me, there must be always one person around that I can talk to, discuss the idea with, and read scenes to as I write them. I need that person as I need a sounding board. I find it very hard to work entirely alone, though I have done so a couple of times. But more than one person is dangerous. Katherine Mansfield used to say that if she told the plot of any of her stories before she had written it, the story felt betrayed and frequently refused, thereafter, to be written at all. That is another of those slightly affected remarks, but I know exactly what she meant. I think the truer explanation is that if she had had the fun of telling the story, all that was left for her was work. The excitement, the sense of "I've got a secret," had gone in the telling, and work without fun is a dreary and unproductive business. There is fun in writing, and a great deal of the fun is the sense of having a surprise up one's sleeve.

There is, too, the problem of what you are to tell, how much you are to tell, how much, even, you are able to tell. The play, as you have seen it in your head and in the way in which it haunts your imagination, has a certain specific appeal for you, it has a magic for you. It is very seldom that that magic can be communicated, except by the actual writing. Recited flatly, it can sound very dull and very silly. I cannot imagine Tennessee Williams being able to describe *The Glass Menagerie* before he had written it, in any way that could communicate its charm and its appeal. It would, surely, have sounded like the most trivial of short stories. A detail could have done the trick, a line of Amanda's dialogue that brought her to life and so redeemed the rest. How much Tennessee Williams could have known this in advance, I cannot guess.

You have to be very sure, too, of your audience, not so much of its intelligence as of its tact. That is why it may be unwise to choose as a listener anyone whom one knows too well. He may not say a word, or any wrong word, but his face as well as his silence can give away his opinion—tact is too difficult among real intimates—and the author is at his most sensitive just then. An ill-chosen word, an apparent lack of enthusiasm, a doubt from the hearer, can kill the author's play for him. The ideal listener, perhaps, should be neither too familiar, nor perhaps even too intelligent, but sensitive and sympathetic, and I hardly need to say that that is a difficult person to find. But a listener you must probably have. The best you can do is to select the best available, remember his shortcomings, try not to imagine that he is thinking more than he says, steel your own sensibility as well you can, and do your best to convey the essence that has enchanted you. It is a very rare writer who can follow the practice of a woman playwright of my acquaintance who can work by herself for six months and more without even her husband's knowing what it is that she is engaged on all day long.

Let us assume now that I am the person to whom you are doing the talking, and that I have asked questions, the questions that I listed above. Those questions open up other questions, as to what I mean when I use those words—theme, story, plot, mood. What are they; how many of them do you need; can you —or must you—have them all at once? Let me start with the theme. That is what your play is about, what it is trying to say. It is akin to that awkward, dangerous and by no means necessary thing, your message. You can state it without telling me the plot or the characters at all. You can state the theme of *The Wild Duck* without mentioning Hjalmar and Hedvig. The theme of that play is the necessity of illusion in the lives of a great many people, and the fact that the man who comes in, insisting on truth for all, is one of those "confounded duns who come pestering us in our poverty with the claims of the ideal." The theme of *Hedda Gabler* is the psychotic effect of frustration, illustrated through a jealous and idle woman. The theme of *Death of a Salesman* is the American dream of Success. The theme of *Othello* is jealousy. I have no idea what the theme of *Hamlet* is. I think most of the world's critics are still trying to find out. I am not at all sure that Shakespeare knew. I suspect that the play and all its terrific content forced itself on him, pouring itself onto paper. Very likely he thought the theme was something far slighter than it seems to us today.

Do you really need a theme? It is a good thing to have one, to be able to analyze what the play is about, what is the thing that you are trying to express, without having to go into plot detail. You must be careful not to be too tied to it, not to stick to it too closely, even to forget it a great deal of the time that you are writing; but it is good to make one serious effort to clarify it to yourself, to state it as briefly and as surely as you can, before you begin. It does not have to be an original theme, or even an unusual one, but it is good to know just where you are aiming, what is the total gesture of the experiences you are planning to record. You can answer, then, and in a few words, the question that will almost certainly be asked of you—the question of what your play is about; what, exactly, you were after. If you are writing about revenge, it is well to know whether you approve of revenge, whether your play will establish that revenge pays or does not pay, or whether you plan to leave that point open. In any case, you know you are going to write about revenge, and you must, presumably, have some attitude toward it. That knowledge alone will help you to keep your lines straight, and it may stop you from writing two acts about revenge and a third about something quite different that may have sprung from your plot. It will help you to keep your theme and plot parallel to each other, to see that they are not contradictory, that they match. Failure to see this spoiled a play for me, I have long thought. *Flowers of the Forest* started from a plot, a bad thing to begin with. Then it developed a theme, and the theme became the more important of the issues. The plot, when it emerged, looked strange, irrelevant and a last-moment makeshift. The theme and the plot never balanced. Watch your theme. It is the play's essence, its total effect, put into as few and as general words as possible. If you cannot find those words, you may still be all right, but watch out. You may also be in danger.

Story; plot; are these the same, and if not, what is the difference between them? This I can answer and swiftly, not from my own knowledge, but from that of E. M. Forster, who outlined it most satisfactorily in his *Aspects of the Novel*. A story, he said, depends on time. "The King died, and then the Queen died." It is a succession of incidents in time. It answers the oldest audience question in the world, the question of: "And then?" Plot depends on causation. "The King died, and then the Queen died of a broken heart." That is a plot. It is not just that the King died on Monday, and the Queen on Tuesday. It answers a deeper audience question, the question of: "And why?" I do not think you can have a plot without a story, but you can have a story without a plot. Most picaresque novels, novels of adventure, and plays adapted from them, have little or no plot. The hero wanders; he meets a man in this place, an old woman in that; he falls in love with a girl and leaves her; he falls in love with another girl, and she leaves him. In the end, he meets another girl, and marries her. This is a story. There is no "why" to be answered. The only answer would be that he kept on moving.

It is far easier to invent a story than to contrive a plot. A good plot needs a special kind of brain to create it. I think that I, myself, am incapable of doing so. It needs a kind of mathematical instinct, a power to tie pieces together, thread incidents so that they lead logically (and unexpectedly) from one to another, and then turn the whole thing into a neat package for the ending. You can do it, or you cannot. If you can, you are liable to become very popular. You will be a successor to the wandering story-teller, to the troubadour, and to Scheherazade. You will tell the whole world bedtime stories. De Maupassant had the gift, so had Kipling, so has Somerset Maugham. Dickens thought he had it, but no one can remember his plots today. Chekhov was without it, entirely. The members of each class are apt to despise slightly the members of the other.

Since I am incapable of devising plots, I too am apt to be a little leery of them. They can hold my attention, make me unable to put down the book or leave the theater, and afterward I forget them. Who wishes to read a detective novel twice? When we were staging *I Remember Mama,* one of the producers came to me with a worry. The play was divided into two acts. When the curtain fell on Act One, one of the small segments of plot had ended. What suspense was there, he asked me, what inducement to the audience to return after the intermission to see what happened next? My answer was that if by that time (an hour and twenty minutes after the curtain rose) we had not interested the audience in our people sufficiently to make it want to come back and see some more about them, I was extremely doubtful whether or not holding over the question of the child's recovery from her mastoid operation would be sufficient to bring it back. I think I was right. But I also think that *I Remember Mama* was something of a special case, being derived from a number of short stories that were linked only by having the same characters.

For the devisers of really ingenious plots, I have an admiration that is not too far away from that which I feel for a good magician or a card-trick expert. Quite often they can even fool me that they are doing better than they really are. Anyone less than the best gives me the feeling that the work is a little on the cheap side. It seems to me that life does not deal very much in plot, and that when it does there is something slightly disgusting about it, as though a devil had got his hand into the machinery. There is the old plot of the man and woman who can only extricate one or the other from a charge of murder by confessing that when the murder happened they were in bed together. That must have happened in real life. It must have been very nasty for the people concerned. But as a plot it makes me a little uncomfortable. I wince under it. It might happen to me, but if it did, I should feel that I had got myself—or had been gotten—into a nasty and also an accidental jam, and I do not think that jams of that kind are worthy of being seriously written about. That kind of plot, too, has about it the faint sound of the author licking his lips over the nasty mess he has managed to get his characters into this time, and it gives the impression of having been constructed backward, from the top scene in reverse, like a mathematical problem.

There have been many plays with plots of this kind, and many of them have been successful, especially those constructed as vehicles for stars. It is the way that movie plots are apt to be invented. I am reminded here of the brilliant critical analysis by C. E. Montague of a play by Sardou, master of such plots, entitled *La Sorcière*. Montague outlines the procedure admirably. "Imagine," he says,

the first germ, the first thought, the very practical thought—"What will make a good harrowing climax for Sarah Bernhardt?" Well, he might start from a standard melodramatic horror—a condemnation of the innocent to death. How, then, to sharpen its poignancy? Make the death burning; that's something. What next? Make her convict herself to save a lover. Good—what next? Make her feel that in killing herself to save her lover, she is merely leaving him in a rival's arms. Excellent!—anything more? Yes, deprive her of the consolation of knowing or hoping that the lover will ever understand her sacrifice or value her memory. That is the way the climax of a tragic machine may be devised, by a cumulative process of invention. The climax once there, the plot issues out of it, backward: each step "disengages" itself. Burning?—that means the time of the Inquisition. A lover who shall be set free at a word from a mistress on trial herself and about to be burnt? Make the lady a Moor, a heathen, the man a Christian Spaniard so framed to please the Holy Office, that they will fairly jump at a chance to let him off. But how shall she be made, while clearing him, to damn herself quite in his eyes? Nothing for it but to make her avow herself, in his hearing, as a witch, and confess she has used hellish arts to make him fall in love with her. Yes, but she must not have verily used hellish art: else where would your audience's sympathy be? And so, of necessity, this Moorish lady of 1517 must practice therapeutic hypnotism in order to scandalize sixteenth-century Toledo, but must also talk twentieth-century science about it so that the audience may know she is only a female Charcot, born rather soon, and not a veritable Witch of Endor. Thus are the unknown terms of Sardou's equation disengaged; the whole of *La Sorcière* follows of its own accord.

I have never seen *La Sorcière,* but I have seen others—and from the same author—that were not unlike it. I do not know whether Montague was correct in guessing that that was how they were written, but it seems more than probable. I can only say that the best plays are not written that way.

All of this is truer today than it used to be. Time was, and not more than thirty years ago, when a good plot was considered essential in the theater. If the need for it has faded, I think that is due quite largely to the movies. The movies exist on plot, as the theater used to. In the first place, they almost never use characters, and neither do real plots. The murder plot can be used for absolutely anyone, or for no one. The movies (and, I suppose, the radio and television) are the modern equivalents of the bedtime story. The old plots get handed down. There was a famous plot which used to do very nicely in the theater. It is the plot (or part of it) of *Madame X,* the mother and the long-lost child who meet dramatically, coincidentally, at a crisis in the lives of one or the other. After its long theater service, it went over to the movies, where it worked wonderfully for many years, providing emotional vehicles for female stars. If it has disappeared of late, I am expecting it in the television dramas next.

One has to watch out for plots, too, and for one's memories of them, and for the occasions when they too conveniently arrive to fill a gap or stop up a hole. They are apt to catch one unaware, stealing up on one. There is the *Tosca* plot, where the woman, in order to save her husband, lover or child, has to submit to the villain's sexual desires. (Perhaps it would be fairer to call it the *Measure for Measure* plot.) It has served for many plays, and made a great success in my youth in the Chinese melodrama, *Mr. Wu.* I was amazed to find, not so many years ago, that Maurice Maeterlinck had employed it in the last act of his play, *Mary Magdalen,* where it is suggested that Jesus might have been saved from crucifixion if Mary had been willing to give herself to the Roman general. This really shocked me a good deal, seeming like a mixture of incense and soda pop. It may well have been memory and inattentiveness on the author's part that let it happen. And to more seriously minded men—especially those who are novelists by profession—there is an odd kind of patronage toward the theater which, when they themselves try it, leads them to believe that it must be somehow below their own level of dignity; that things have to be "souped up," to use John Marquand's phrase; and that plots, such as come out of their far-back memory of eighteen-ninety dramas, are still essentials. The same thing happens with playwrights when they are hired to write movies.

This is an odd thing, this mixture of envy and contempt. It betokens the idea on which I happened when I started this book, the idea of the theater as a perishable or ephemeral form of art, and the resultant stooping toward it. The authors, for all their wish to participate (which I would guess to be due one-third to envy of the money and publicity, one-third to a slightly ashamed personal enjoyment of the theater in the past, and one-third to a longing to see their own creations in action), cannot help feeling that there is a certain cheapness about it, a lessening of standards, and that, therefore, it can be managed with less skill and less care than they would give to their own work. Nothing could be further from the truth. Perishable and ephemeral though the form may seem to be, it has its own rules, its own technique, and it can absorb a lifetime of devoted attention and love before it will yield up its secrets. It cannot be condescended to. The authors are apt to find that out when they embark on it, and then to retire discouraged, hurt and a little more contemptuous than when they embarked. The theater has taken its revenge on them. That is sad. We need these men in it badly. Very few have combined both talents. John Galsworthy, Somerset Maugham and J. B. Priestley are almost the only ones whose names jump to my mind as being equally successful as novelists and playwrights. J. M. Barrie deserted novel-writing for the theater.

Recently, Carson McCullers performed the difficult job of

converting her own novel, *The Member of the Wedding,* into a successful play. And she did it, I would say, by a total absorption in her subject, with no regard for the theatrical conventions beyond a wish to use the stage as best she could. That the play was successful, there is no doubt. That I, myself, found it enormously absorbing, there is also no doubt. A number of people declined to accept it, deciding that it was no play. That is a way out of a great many awkward situations. It was used for many years against Bernard Shaw, to cover his successes by people who found them distasteful. It is certain that *The Member of the Wedding* broke a number of rules, did a number of things all wrong, some, even, quite badly. It had a theme—the theme of personal loneliness—it had no plot (except between scenes in the last act), and almost no story. It hardly moved for more than two acts. What put it over, what was the quality which made it so enchanting, and so deeply moving to me? I think the quality of the last word in the questions that I used above—the quality of mood.

If there is a new-born creature in the theater of the past thirty years, I would say that it is the play of mood, the play whose main quality—far more important than its story or its plot—is the maintenance and communication of a certain mood, through which the entire action is presented. There are not a great many of them, and Carson McCullers' is one of the best. *The Glass Menagerie* is another. To the people trained in an older theater, it looks as though the authors were totally unable to write in dramatic form at all, just as the paintings of many of the French impressionists of the eighties and nineties conveyed the same impression as regards drawing.

Where did this new kind of play start? I think that I caught one of the earliest glimpses of it in the description of a play which my parents saw at the London Stage Society around 1911. My mother told me—and she was an intelligent woman, deeply grounded in Ibsen and the classics—that it was either completely insane, or else that the whole audience was. It was by a Russian playwright, and it was called *The Cherry Orchard*. For many years after, I regarded Chekhov as many people regard Gertrude Stein. I did not see the play myself, nor read it, until about fourteen years later. In the interim, I had come to hear and accept other judgments of Chekhov. The strangeness had already started to pass away from him.

Why was that play so different from its predecessors that it must have seemed as though it were written on a totally different tone-scale, so that neither form nor melody was apparent then, just as the music of Wagner, followed by Strauss, Debussy and Stravinsky, seemed incomprehensible to ears familiar with Handel, Gounod and Verdi? I can only think it was in the absence of plot or definitive story-line, of star parts or organized build. The play concentrated on a conception of people seen in their personal relationships, just as such, and not for what theatrically emerged from them. It was not written to any specific climax; there was no organized gathering of forces; ultimately, the essential thing was the mood in which it was conceived and performed. If that went over, if the audience was able to catch it, share it, be moved by it, then the author had made the impression he desired. If not, then the evening was about nothing at all, and either the author was insane or the whole audience was.

I am under the impression that the 1911 production of *The Cherry Orchard* was not a good one, that neither the director nor the company really had too clear an idea of what they were aiming at. This may well have helped the confusion, but it did not make it. The play itself was too different from most things the public had been used to. If the taste changed speedily, we must remember the year. From 1914 on, almost everything changed speedily. The whole world changed. Manners changed, morals changed, the whole tempo of life altered forever. It has been said of late by a first-class dramatic critic that Chekhov and Ibsen are themselves old-fashioned nowadays. If I cannot myself quite believe that, it may well be due to my own age. The critic in question is a man whom I believe to be ten years younger than I am. Ibsen wrote plays that were technical miracles; he threw out the trimmings, and concentrated rigidly on his dramatic purpose. His plays are superlatively well-made. They are also a great deal more than that, but their construction set a whole new kind of method in motion. From Ibsen our playwrights learned the trick of communicating what the characters were thinking without having to fall back into soliloquy and aside. People stopped reading letters aloud to themselves on the stage. I still think that no playwright can really know his job, can really dare to try to write a play, unless he knows his Ibsen very well.

Chekhov performed another kind of revolution. Ibsen had cleared the way almost too well. Chekhov re-established the trimmings that Ibsen had rejected, but he used them quite differently. They were no longer embroidery, as they had previously been; they became the play. The play, its characters and their detailed lives and thoughts, were one single thing. He reintroduced something very close to the soliloquy—the speech of characters made in the presence of another, to which that other pays no attention. We can never be quite sure whom the speaker is addressing, but the lonely heart is speaking, and it speaks in tones of music, set in a minor key. The whole of Chekhov is set in a minor key. The mood is a wistful and declining one. It is deeply moving. And—how much this is due to history, I do not know—it is the mood of a tragic swan song of a civilization. To our ears today, *The Cherry Orchard* is even more touching, more alarming, more prophetic than it could have been to those who knew it before the Russian Revolution of 1917.

The author who is telling me the basis of the play he wants to write may well have learned from Chekhov, and from the newer imitators. He may not have a plot or a story, or if he has, those will seem unimportant to him. He may have only a mood, a thing of all most hard to describe or communicate other than through his actual writing. But if it has excited him, if he himself is deeply moved by it, then that will be apparent. He has in many ways the most difficult of all tasks, because the field is almost too clear for him. Working within limits is an easier thing than working with none. Sonnets, as G. K. Chesterton has said, are easier to write than other verse because they are more restricted; there is a severe framework to hold one in. Earlier playwrights have set the general mold, but the mood playwright is largely on his own. Yet he is moving the theater forward, where it needs to go, away from the story and plot play, altering and widening the shape of the proscenium arch. And that is all to the good.

CHAPTER FOUR

Where the Play Comes From

WHERE DID that idea, that you want to write, that you need to write, come from? How did it first strike you? That is a question that is hard, sometimes impossible, to answer. It did not come from looking for it. No amount of search is going to give you that play idea, or any idea truly worth writing. It happens to you, and you may well not always recognize it when it happens. But the moment of conception has occurred. Somewhere, in the creative cells of your being, the germinative process has started. Often, afterward, you look back to see what started it. Sometimes you can remember, sometimes you cannot.

"Where do you authors start your ideas? Do they start from plot or from character?" Those are the traditional questions. The answers must be different from all authors, but I would say, for me at any rate, that the ideas start with characters, and that it is wiser and better that they do. Quite often they start from a phrase of dialogue, a brief remark spoken or remembered, that continues to turn in my head. *The Distaff Side* started from a remark made to me by an aunt, or, rather, reported to me by an aunt. She was my mother's younger sister, and she had never been well off in her financial life. After my mother's death, she told me of a time when my mother (a widow, then) was packing to go abroad for a winter in Italy. My aunt was with her, and was envying her her holiday, her clothes, her freedom to depart. My mother turned to her and said: "And yet I'd change places with you tomorrow." "With me?" my aunt replied. "What have I got?" "You've got your husband," was my mother's answer.

Those lines stayed with me. They haunted my imagination. From them, the whole fabric of the play was created, all the women in that family, representing different phases of a woman's life. The three sisters became as real to me as . . . and there a very odd thing has happened. I was about to write, "as Chekhov's *Three Sisters.*" I will still write it, though aware now of its oddness. I should have written, "as my mother and her two sisters." That would have been the logical thing to say. Those were real women. I knew them well. But they did not, do not, seem as real to me as Olga, Masha and Irina in the play that, I think, I would rather have been able to write than any play in the world. This suggests another remark that was made to me, by my mother when she was worrying over my total preoccupation with the theater, in my early twenties. "You are so absorbed in it," she said, "that I begin to think that people in plays, and the things that happen to them, are more real and more important to you than the people and incidents of real life." I did not deny this criticism. It was true. In many ways it is still true. Chekhov's *Three Sisters* are almost more real to me than my mother and my aunts. I know that I know them better.

I carried the idea for *The Distaff Side* for a long time, for almost two years, needing a fragment of plot on which to hang it. That, also, came by accident. I heard of a young actress whose fiancé came to her one day with the news that he had obtained a job with a touring company that was going to Australia for a year, and that he wanted her to marry him and go too. When she hesitated, he said: "Either you marry me now, this week, or the engagement is off." It seemed to me that that situation would suffice to provide a peg for all the things that my play was to say. I think it did, but I still think that "suffice" is the only word to use. The play, the gist and basis of the play, turned on all the things concerning my own mother, and from her concerning all women, things relating to marriage and a woman's sense of purpose in her life, that were in the remark that my aunt had reported to me. The girl's story was something on which to hang them, and no more. The remark reported by my aunt is still in the script, a main turning point in it. That does not always happen. Quite often, the thing that started the play can become the one thing that has subsequently to be left out. This is not necessarily a fault. It can mean that the imagination has gone ahead on its own, springing from and then by-passing the initial starting place. But when it does last, without having to be dragged in, it shows that the imagination was right from the beginning.

I could outline the first phrases that started a good many of my plays. *After All* came from a day when I was feeling rather good and successful, and was driving in a taxi past the college where my mother used to go. I saw girls arriving there then, and

I can remember thinking: "Mother as a girl. I wonder if she ever thought of me then." That may not sound like a very good beginning for a play, but it was how that one started, and there, too, the remark stayed in the script. Another play came from staring at the outside of a big house in an old-fashioned slummy district in London, and trying to visualize the life inside. Some plays I have wholly now forgotten the beginnings of. I cannot remember at all what made me think of the slightly original idea of *Bell, Book and Candle,* and that made me want to write about modern witches. But all the ideas started tiny, as one cell only, and the cell grew until it became a play.

That is how I think that a play should happen, and for a while, after the initial thought has made its necessary first click, the author should do nothing but allow it to grow of its own volition, letting the play cocoon itself around that thought, even—in Robert Graves's phrase—pretending that he does not care too much about it, masking his hunger, letting it seem small matter if it come or stay. Once you are sure, quite, quite sure, that it is solidly there, then comes the time for work.

There are other factors in this matter of the choice of, or of being chosen by, one's idea. They are factors that depend on one's consciousness, or one's subconsciousness, at the time. One is not always aware of them. My own first decent (I mean, dramatically decent) preoccupation was with my home, and my resentments toward it. I have shown that from the sketch that I have given of my own first halfway decent manuscript. I am interested now—now that the years have moved on—to notice that in that, as well as in several other playscripts, and in a number of short stories, the emphasis was always laid on the father-and-son relationship, the misunderstandings and the lack of outward sympathy between them, and a need—usually fulfilled —for the dispersal of that feeling. This was not outwardly my own case at all. I was not on very good terms with my father. He died when I was eighteen, and I was not consciously aware that I had missed a friendly relationship with him. It was my mother that I was fonder of. Yet the mother plays very little, if any, part in these earlier ideas. It is always the father. I finally succeeded in managing a good expression of that obsessing emotion in my play, *Young Woodley*. (In that play a phrase occurs that I remember my father using to me as a reproof for a piece of dramatic self-pity on my part. "Don't try heroics on. They won't wash," he said. I have been surprised to find this also in the earlier script I have described.) The scene between Woodley and his father, who appears in the last act only, seems to me a very good one still. After *Woodley* I tried it again, in a larger form, in a play called *Diversion*. Here, the situation was a good deal more melodramatic and a good deal less sound. (There was a reason for this. I wrote *Diversion* more or less to order, and with a deadline of date, and can still remember that deadline as one of the most alarming obstacles to creation I have ever experienced. I will never face writing a play with a deadline again.) It is interesting to me now to examine *Diversion* from my present point of view. The play ends with the father—a noted surgeon—giving his son a phial of poison with which to commit suicide and so cheat the police and the hangman. What interests me in this situation is not so much its theatrical vulgarity, as the fact that that was the last time I worked on the father-and-son situation. It was as though that suicide had satisfied whatever basic need, whatever desire or frustration had previously existed in my nature.

After that I turned to mothers. (There was a father in the next play, but his relationship was with his daughter, and he died after Act One.) In *After All* I achieved a portrait of my own mother (also dead by then), in which I used almost only the most tiresome qualities of self-pity and self-martyrdom that I could assemble from her. It was a bitter portrait, though I still think it was humorous and well observed. And some years later, as though overcome by guilt at its unfairness, I did a second picture of my mother, this time only favorable and flattering in its aspects. I still like to think of these two women—Mrs. Thomas in *After All,* and Evie Millward in *The Distaff Side*— as being among the better characters that I have written, although I think they might have been even better still as one figure, had I had the detachment to be able to achieve that, then. And, after Evie Millward, I stopped writing mothers as the main figures in my plays, too. The father in *Diversion* had enabled his son to commit suicide, Evie had helped to set her daughter free for a better vision of living than she had previously had. Both my parents had triumphed now in some way, and I was through with them as a creator.

From family plays, I moved on to other things. I was still drawing largely on my own background. It has been said that a writer's material is dependent on what has happened to him by the age of twenty-five. I think—or like to think—that that is a slight exaggeration, but there is a lot of truth in it. For every writer, too, there is a period of time which any experience needs before it can be translated into the subject matter for work. The amount of time varies not only with every author, but also with every experience. (The subject matter of *The Voice of the Turtle* took only a few weeks.) Miss Sheila Kaye-Smith has stated that with her it is usually about four years, and I would say that that is a fairly accurate figure for most authors and for most ideas. A digestive process has to go on before the idea can emerge in its new form.

These predilections of the spirit, or of the subconscious, in regard to what a play is to be about are worth trusting. In fact, they are almost the only thing worth trusting, because it is from that level that one writes. They have little connection with reason, and that is wise, too. Reason can be of help, must be of help, in the actual writing of the work, but the basic desire comes from a deeper region. It comes from the same region from which one falls in love, and in which one's religious beliefs are rooted. The psyche chooses what it wants to express. That is why I have never thought very much of notebooks, at any rate, of notebooks for themes. If a theme is so elusive that it cannot be trusted to remain without a note being taken of it, it cannot have its roots very deep in one's inside. I have never cared much for notebooks, anyway. I have almost never used anything that I have made a note of. I cannot help feeling that notebooks are a way of being rude to one's subconscious.

It is from the subconscious that one creates. If it approves of one's work, of the subject one has chosen, then it will do all kinds of hands' turns for one, will present one with all manner of surprising and unexpected gifts, so that one will be continually amazed by the things that come from the typewriter. If it does not approve, it will merely go to sleep, leaving one to do all the work oneself. And that work is seldom satisfactory. Rebecca West has made all this clear in the superb essays in her book, *The Strange Necessity*, which should be read by every author. It will tell him exactly what his work, his job and his whole artistic life are about.

The reason, the intelligence, are bad guides for the choice of material. This is how so many poor propaganda plays have come to be written. The author was impressed by his subject matter, feeling that his play was a call to deliverance, but the impression was on his brain and his mind, and most often not in his heart. The plays seem specious and empty when they come to us. The creative side has not been operating, and the subconscious has gone to sleep. Watch out for plays that seem to prove a theme too closely, of which the theme can be carefully stated with a logical development. The reason has had too much power there.

There is another serious problem, the problem of the audience. To what extent, if any, should the author take that into consideration in choosing his material? Will he be branded, or can he brand himself, as commercial, if he does so? Will he have fallen below the proper standard of being an artist, if he does? Let us look at this thing reasonably. A play is written, normally, with the intention that it shall be performed. It should please an audience. (As a playwright once said to me: "We want to have the largest audience we can, without sacrificing our self-respect.") The viewpoint of the audience must, therefore, to some extent, be considered. The extent of that extent is something to be argued. If the author is aware that his subject matter will antagonize an audience, or bore it, then he has been warned, and it seems to me to be up to him to take whatever steps he can (again without losing his self-respect) to overcome those objections. Otherwise, his play will remain typed between covers. It will not be quite alive.

There are a number of things that can displease an audience. To some extent, the author is a part of that audience, and will know what those things are. For the most part, a man is unlikely to want to write a play recommending incest between a brother and sister. But he may just possibly feel that he has invented a correct situation to recommend it in, or it may strike him forcibly as a romantic dream. He will almost certainly know, from the ordinary conversations of his daily life, that the average audience will not share that dream, and that he will have a great deal of trouble in persuading it to. If he goes ahead and writes it after that, I incline to think him a little foolish. A play thoroughly recommending crime (in a serious way) would have the same reception. These are the general bases of total disapproval. There are others, some more or less temporary. A play recommending homosexuality, or taking a tolerant view of it (not regarding it as a form of sickness), would be hard of acceptance. That may not last forever. If the author has a firm conviction on the subject, a firm and basic desire to write that play, then he should do so. A play recommending Communism has little, if any, chance of acceptance now. It would have had, ten or fifteen years ago.

When Granville Barker wrote *Waste*, illegal operations (even if the heroine died of them) were impossible of mention on the stage. Barker knew that fact. He went ahead and wrote his play. He knew, too, that it could almost certainly get a production from the London Stage Society, a highly esteemed and deeply valuable organization, which helped to meet just such cases as this. (He also knew that, under his name, it could be printed and read.) The same thing was true of Shaw's *Mrs. Warren's Profession*. It was banned by the censor, and was then produced by the Stage Society. (A quite famous critic wrote of it a remark too little known, and too surprising to be omitted here. "It was an exceedingly uncomfortable afternoon," he said. "For there was a majority of women to listen to that which could only be understood by a minority of men." The play, you will remember, was about the keeping of brothels and the making of an income from them, though the word "brothel" itself was never used.) Shaw had to write that play. It begged and urged him to, and the popular reaction against its subject matter was something that he knew he had to fight. That is ultimately the only answer. Will you feel as though an unborn child were stifling you if you do not write it? Then you must go ahead and deliver it. You have been unfortunate, perhaps, in the theme that has presented itself to you so urgently, but you may also be a prophet in the end. But be sure of that urgency, be sure it is not mere stubbornness. If you are truthful, there is no mistaking it.

The situation can operate in a change of mood in the public against what it might well have accepted earlier, or in the changed conditions of the world. It has seemed sad to me that one of Sidney Howard's finer plays, *Ned McCobb's Daughter,* should be of so much less interest now because it is about prohibition. Once prohibition ceased to be a national institution, the play's effect dwindled. Maxwell Anderson has said that some of his own earlier dramas he would not now allow to be revived, because of the present state of political consciousness. He feels that they would look too much as though he were recommending insubordination to authority, even though the authorities to which he was objecting when he wrote the plays were crooked and perverse, and he still sees them as such. A general sense of danger, a temporary modification of the point of view of freedom, has made him feel that the plays are unwise now. This may seem like temporizing, but the mood of the moment's public has a great deal to do with one's play's reception.

The Voice of the Turtle, written and produced during the war, was timed to an audience exactly in the mood to receive it, and I had astonishingly few letters objecting to its morality. (I cannot think what my mother would have said of it.) In England, a few years later, it met with an audience in a totally different frame of mind. The sense of romance that the war had given the story had disappeared. The appeal was no longer there. Robert Sherwood wrote his war play, *There Shall Be No Night,* at a time when Russia invaded Finland. The Russians were the villains of the play. Later, Germany invaded Russia. The Russians became our allies. The play was impossible, though Sherwood rewrote it in another setting for its European production. It could, actually, go on being rewritten with the participants changing for every single war. It might have been better to set it in an imaginary country, with an unnamed enemy, but audiences are not too fond of that kind of play, or at any rate of taking it seriously. Sherwood was unfortunate, though Russia could return to being the villain now.

There was a time (I think it was in the nineteen-thirties) when Shakespeare's *Coriolanus* was forbidden production in Paris, because the contemporary mood of the politically minded public would see it as an incentive to fascism. If it can happen to Shakespeare, it can happen to anyone. If one is aware of the situation in advance, one's courage, one's independence, and one's political sense can be the only guides. In almost all cases, the drive of the play and of its idea will be the deciding factors.

CHAPTER FIVE

Construction and Scenario

THE IDEA has been turning itself about in your head, accumulating other things around it, without your conscious intervention, and now it looks as if it could make a play. Now is the time when real work has got to start, when reason and experience must be brought into action. They cannot stand off now any longer.

What happens next is, I will frankly admit, the period I hate most. I detest planning a play. I dislike the sense of construction to the point of hating even to use the word. It suggests to me a form of dreary mechanics. I know of other playwrights to whom this period is the happiest time of all. I can only speak for myself. I am restless and bothered and deeply unhappy. I go for walks, take long drives in the car. These occupations use my body sufficiently for me not to be aware of it, and therefore set my mind free. Neither the walk nor the drive should be very interesting, and the walk should not be uphill, or I become conscious of my body again. Once, a long time ago, I went to Fontainebleau in France to think out a play. For the first two days, I walked in the forest. It was beautiful, and it was disturbing. The play got nowhere. On the third day, I discovered a walk right in the town. It took about an hour, never leaving sight of houses, and it went by the railway. I took that walk twice a day for three days, and the play was ready to be put on paper. There had been nothing that I saw to distract my attention.

There is another aspect to this period of planning which is hard to describe. It involves a need to forget what one is doing, that one is trying to construct a play. The process must take a hold of its own. I took a long drive a few years ago, with a play idea ready to be thought out. The roads where I live, down in the California desert, are straight and empty, and they do not have stop signs. I drove for almost half an hour without being aware that I was driving, or that I was thinking in terms of scenes. I did not consciously know that I was doing anything. I was getting along fine. Then I approached a small town; there was a stop sign; I obeyed it, and instantly I became aware of myself again. I knew what I had been up to, that I was planning a play, and it took a long while before I could return to it with any kind of success.

That self-forgetfulness is of great importance. I could guess at a number of reasons for it. The best of them is that the self, the awareness of self as a creator, or a writer, or even as a participant, gets in the way of true expression. The more plays one has written, the greater is the danger of remembering that self, its past, its reputation, the things that friends and critics have said. The sense of oneself stands like a great block in the way of surrender to the work itself. Spiritually, I could say that the text of "I can of mine own self do nothing" is of value in explaining this. The great need is a total submergence of that self and of that self's involvement, a submission to the idea and to what is called inspiration. There is not much point in advocating it. The more one tells another, or oneself, to forget himself, the harder it is to do. It is like trying to make the mind a blank, to think of nothing. As long as one remembers that instruction, the mind continues to play with the idea that it is thinking about nothing and continues to repeat that phrase, so that it is thinking not of nothing, but of thinking of nothing, which is not the same thing.

There is another reason for the distaste that I have for this period, a reason that has nothing to do with laziness or distaste for work. This is the period when you can make mistakes that can prove fatal, and you will never know what they are until it is too late to do anything about them, if you ever know them at all. The construction of a play sets up its shape, and builds its skeleton. It is probably at this moment that the ultimate fate of the play is settled. Polishing, rewriting, tackling bits here and there, all the trimming and technique, all the things that will happen from here on, before, during and after the rehearsals, can help you only if your play is basically sound. If it is not, they will not be able to do a thing for you. This is the moment when the humpback or the brachycephalic head can happen, and you will learn that no make-up can cover those from showing, later on. It is here and now that you have to be sure. Is it any wonder, then, that I am scared of this time in the life of a play?

I would like to take a play subject, and illustrate some of the constructional problems that can happen to it. Let me take the plot of *Cinderella* as a starting point. You have just thought of the main outline: the daughter of a rich family, oppressed and treated as a slave in the household of her remarried father; the ugly sisters; the ball; the godmother; the heroine's flight at midnight; the incident with the slipper, and the happy ending. Now, with that in your mind, you have to start to plan it. You know, presumably, from what angle you are going to write it. There are several. It could even be a propaganda play, with Cinderella and the Prince as liberals, and the sisters, and presumably the King, as reactionary capitalists. This would need a special setting-up. There might have to be a scene between the Prince and his father, almost at the start of the play. There would probably have to be a meeting between Cinderella and the Prince, with their identities unknown to each other, in the first act. Perhaps they would discuss the general political situation, and the traditional Court attitude toward it. They might even discuss the ball, though there is a difficulty here. Cinderella must want to go to the ball. It ought to be a romantic occasion for her, though the whole story can be switched, so that she wants to go merely to make a protest, or to write an article on it, deploring its extravagance. You can see how the play is beginning to change?

All of this may sound facetious. It was not my intention to make it so. Let us go back to the story, and assume that it is to be told romantically, as a straight, dream-fulfillment plot. The first thing involved will be the establishment of Cinderella and her position in the house. This will be easy. A brief scene with the sisters will do that for you. (I am omitting the step-

mother, who seems to me to add little, and to clutter the stage.)
Cinderella, herself, will need putting over. She must have someone to talk to, to explain herself to. This might well be her
father, who can be either a cruel man (unwise, if the sisters
are cruel too), or a bullied, defeated, helpless man whose life
has got out of his hands. I see a character forming here. I can
see scenes between him and the daughter he would like to help,
but no longer knows how to. I can see his spasmodic efforts,
beaten and forgotten. These scenes, however, reveal the father
rather than Cinderella. Perhaps she will need another compan-
ion, to whom she can speak more freely. The English panto-
mimes on the subject used to have a character called Buttons,
who was mainly comic relief. A more modern and gentler version of Buttons, perhaps in love with Cinderella, might help
here. He is the boy-of-all-work in a rather impoverished household. The details of its poverty can be either humorous or touching. Make up your mind now; it will be too late later on. Buttons
is poorly fed, but he shares his rations with Cinderella. Watch
out for the political angle, again.

I can now see the household established. The aged father,
the wicked sisters, the lovelorn page boy, and Cinderella herself. Cinderella is still vague to me. She has to be the heroine,
she has to be sympathetic, but she needs clarification. What are
her main interests in life? They can be animals, of course, which
suggests that she will talk to the cat or the dog, and that brings
up another problem. Are we going to have talking cats and dogs
in the play? It is still a fairy story, of course, but is that going too
far? You will have to make up your mind about that, too. It
can set the whole shape of your play for you. Perhaps you would
rather that she is sympathetic to mice, and that that is why they

are willing to help serve her later on, because she has always stood out against traps for them. You will have a scene about traps. But do audiences like mice? Women are supposed to be afraid of them. The actors will not be able to look like mice, really. How wise is this? Another problem is opening up.

But there is a bigger problem. The Prince. He is the hero. When does he appear? Not until the ball? That is late. It is not necessarily too late. The Archduke Rudolph does not appear in *Reunion in Vienna* until Act Two. That suggests something else. Can the Prince, who is a dummy character so far, be made to resemble Rudolph, a man "constantly intoxicated with his own charm"? Can the whole story be turned to resemble *Reunion in Vienna,* and Cinderella's flight at the end of Act Two be made to ensure her own unwilling safety from the Prince's amorous advances? Yes, it can. To write such a plot would mean omitting all the magic, all the fairy-story element; the godmother would become like Frau Lucher, a kind of procuress; the whole thing takes on instantly a new kind of sophistication. You can see again how the play can shift its ground under you right now.

But to write such a plot would also give it too strong a reminiscent quality. It is wiser to forget it. Go back to where you started, with the magic play. It will be better if the Prince can appear in Act One. Does that mean that the first act will have to have two scenes, one in the Palace, to create the Prince, and his failure to find a girl who pleases him, and one in the Cinderella home? That will do, but it divides the play up, and it still separates the two leads. It does not seem like a very good idea. It would be better to have the two meet in Act One, and again they had better not know who the other is. This is easy for the

Prince. Cinderella can easily pass as the scullery maid, though it makes a scene between them hard to establish, unless that fact stirs his interest in her, and in her bad clothes and general under-nourishment. Again, the political impact is starting. Perhaps it cannot be kept out. But who does she think he is? He can be traveling incognito, under another name. What is he doing there? I assume "there" to be the Cinderella home. Can he be an amateur artist or decorator, anxious to make comic sketches of the sisters or drawings of the shapes of the old castle rooms? These do not sound too good. Perhaps the animals are a better bet. He is out on a walk with his dog, and the dog has got a thorn in its paw, and he stops here to borrow a pair of tweezers. Cinderella supplies them, pulls out the thorn, and an interest springs up between them. This is not very good, but it is getting some-where. At least, we have got the Prince on stage in Act One.

Your next problem will be where you should drop your first-act curtain. It can fall after the godmother has appeared, has done her work and dressed Cinderella for the ball. This puts a great deal into Act One. That is nothing against it, so long as there is enough left for Act Two. In that case, Act Two will be the ball. You will have a hard time staging that, for reasons I will explain later. But even if you do, will there be quite enough material to go around? The scene between Cinderella and the Prince has some meat under it now, if she knows who he is, but he does not recognize her as the girl he met that morning. (Was it morning? Could it be that afternoon? In any case, the time element is starting to make trouble. We have to see the sisters dressing for the ball—that is one of the basic things that started you on the play, the vision of that scene. Can it all be tied into one undivided act? Will a curtain not have to be dropped to

mark the passage of a few hours?) But in any case, their conversation is not likely to sustain a whole act. The ball will do
for a scene, but hardly for an act.

Very well, then. You start to go backward. You will end your
first act when the sisters go to the ball, and Cinderella is left
alone and unhappy. A short scene with Buttons, who perhaps
offers marriage. She is nice to him, and sends him away. The
curtain will fall on her lonely figure, or else on the entrance of
the godmother. Something else to decide here. Should the godmother be planted or prepared for in the first act? Should Cinderella know that she has a godmother? It will be very easy for
Father to have explained her. He could have been very fond of
her once, hoped perhaps for a romance with her, but after he
remarried (why?), she went away and never came back. I can
see a good scene springing from this, though Father is starting
to run away with the play. In any case, you decide it is best to
put Act Two into two scenes. In the first, Cinderella is prepared
for the ball, and the pumpkin and the mice are turned into a
coach and horses. You will worry now whether all this can be
done on stage, or whether it will have to be managed off. If it
has to be off, then Cinderella must watch and describe it, unless
you bring Buttons back to do so. He may very well be quite useful as an adjunct to the preparation scene, can fetch and carry
things. There may be some value in his seeing Cinderella in her
ball gown, too, and in his being awed by her.

Then Scene 2 will be the ball. You will have to use Father
and the sisters again here. This will need some management.
You may have to go back and establish an old friendship between Father and the King, or else the Prime Minister, in order
to get a scene between them. In that case, could Cinderella and

the Prince have known each other and played together as children? When they meet in Act One, can the Prince have heard falsely that she was dead, and talk to the girl he thinks is the slavey about her, while Cinderella keeps her mouth shut on the subject? Then when he sees her now, he sees her as he would have imagined the dead Cinderella to have grown up to look. Perhaps he taxes her with it, asks her if she is not the child he used to know. The godmother has warned her that she must not reveal her true identity, so again she spars with him. Another Sherwood play is creeping in here. There is a strong resemblance to *Idiot's Delight* in that situation.

If you have trouble filling up Act Two, you will be tempted to a drunk scene. You will always be tempted to a drunk scene. Who gets drunk? Father? Not if you have made him a pathetic figure. Then one or both of the sisters will have too much champagne, and a whole comedy routine can come out of that. (A whole second act has been known to be made of it.) Cinderella and the Prince may come in on the end of it. Their amusement, their efforts to help, will provide a background for their scene together. Perhaps they finish the champagne and start into a love scene. Then the clock strikes, just as sex is willingly approaching, and Cinderella flies, leaving her slipper (has the Prince been drinking out of it?) behind for him to find.

Act Three is an easy act. That is one of the things that had endeared the story to you. It has a climax already made. You will need only some invention as to suspense, to holding off Cinderella's appearance to try on the slipper, and after that everything will go smoothly. You will have things to straighten out. You cannot leave Father and Buttons out in the cold. Their stories will have to be finished off, now that you have started them. The farewell scene between Buttons and Cinderella will be a useful and touching one. Father must be taken care of, and made happy. Anything else that you have invented—such as any political issues—will have to be rounded off, too. The loose ends will have to be tidied up. One of these will be what is going to happen to the sisters? Cinderella, naturally, has no heart for revenge. A heroine must not have. The Prince would probably like to see them punished, but he, as hero, may not achieve it either. Yet the audience will feel revengeful, and will not suffer the sisters to go free. You cannot cheat the audience out of that satisfaction. But you must not be too cruel; we have got beyond the days of Grimm. This may need some further preparation from the beginning, to prepare the exactly right degree of revenge on them. This subject of revenge will be taken up again later, too.

There, very briefly, is an indication of some of the construction problems. I have chosen an easy story. The only real problem is the handling of the Prince, and of how to make him a good part. Everything else falls into place fairly easily, though once you start to create characters for Cinderella and the Prince, you may find further problems developing. Nothing ever stands quite still, or lets a play stand still. It will take you along with it, and you have to watch where. From all this, you will see the shape of your play emerging. There are half a dozen other ways of handling it. It can be done in a number of short scenes like *Dinner at Eight*. It can be worked with scrims and soliloquies and scenes that are played in the imagination only. It can be done in verse, and it can be a high and chic comedy. Now is the time to find out. Now is the time to settle which it is going to be. Once settled, you will not be able to go back. The play's shape and its figure will have become established, and from then on you will be stuck with them. All you can do after that is to dress and re-dress them, but the bones will stay the same.

From now on, you are going to have to start a more detailed form of planning. Let us forget Cinderella now, and return to that unknown play that you had started to tell me about. Where do you begin that planning? Perhaps with a scene, an especial scene, if possible in the first act, and how one can best lead up to and away from it. Or you can start at the beginning, and try to decide what time of day it is, the time of day that will enable your characters to come on and off naturally, giving them long enough time to stay on stage and a good reason for leaving when you want them to go. That involves deciding on the set, where it is, whose house it is. From one of those points of departure, the play should start to move.

Should one prepare a scenario? Should it all be written out in advance? That depends entirely on the author. I never like to write anything down, but I know of other playwrights who have to have it on paper. One, especially, likes to list the succession of scenes with a rough time limit, described in the number of pages, that each will take. "Act One. George's Apartment. Afternoon. George is preparing cocktails. Enter Paul. Scene for Paul and George, planting George's engagement to Mary— three pages. Enter Mary. Scene for Paul, George and Mary— mainly introduction—one page. George has to go out and buy liquor. Scene for Paul and Mary—five pages." That is fine, but it does not work for me. In any case, even the playwrights who employ it have admitted that it usually gets changed a great deal while they are working. But it serves as a basis on which to start. A few complete and total scenarios have been written, and I can remember having read one printed in a book somewhere. I can also remember thinking that I did not see what fun the playwright was going to have when he came to start writing the play. But perhaps he was one of those to whom that period is never fun. For me, it is the best time in the world, the time when I am actually writing, and the dialogue is flowing and starting to surprise me, and even the whole brief scenario as I had planned it is starting to change and mold itself better and better for me, because the characters are true and alive now.

That "whole brief scenario" that I have mentioned there, and that I will never write down, just what is it, how complete is it? It is, actually, the least that I can get away with. You cannot sit down and start a play without knowing where you are going. I wish to God that you could. The last line—or the content of the last act—must be in your head before you can begin. Otherwise, you will end nowhere, in a dead rut. You must know roughly what each act will contain, where the stresses are, what the curtains will be, or what they will indicate. You should know your act divisions, feel the whole build of the play, though you need not know it all in detail. By now, I am inclined to be sure enough of myself so that I need to plan only one act ahead in detailed construction. The others, I am inclined to believe, will follow on. But that first act must be fairly clear. I must know the things I have outlined in the fragment of a scenario above. I must know that if it is essential that Mary and Paul have a scene together, in which they can discuss things that George must not hear about, they will have to be left alone together, and I will try to think up a better excuse for George's leaving them than that of having him go out for liquor.

Men do not normally give a cocktail party and not have

liquor in the place. It is perfectly true that that can happen, or that the man from the liquor store can be delayed in arriving. It is true, but it is not likely; it is too convenient, and that is an important thing to watch. Audiences are smart, and they are getting smarter day by day. They will notice that convenience, they will know why the liquor man is late, and know that it is only to suit you, the playwright. They will start to smile or to fidget, and you will know that they do. You must try to think up a better reason for removing George from the stage, a reason they will not realize is a reason for removing him. It should be a reason connected with the plot or the characters, or both. It should seem so normal that they will not notice that he has gone, and that you have the stage all clear. I cannot, at this moment, give you one. But there is one, and you have to go on working and thinking until you have found it.

It gets harder every year, because, as I have said, audiences get smarter all the time. I could give many examples of this need for finding better and better reasons, but I will content myself with one only. This is the opening of *The Second Mrs. Tanqueray*. Here, Aubrey Tanqueray, a widower, is giving a dinner party to three male friends, one of whom has failed to turn up. Aubrey explains to the others why he has called them together, which is because he is about to marry again. He will not tell them who the lady is. Then, as they are all about to go out together somewhere, he asks if they would mind if he writes a couple of notes, adding that he may otherwise forget to do so. He takes a seat at a desk upstage, and starts to write the notes, while the two men talk. These are characters who never appear again in the play, and the fact that I can never forget their names is due partly to the fact that the names are odd ones (Jayne and

Misquith), and more so to the fact that they have always seemed to me to represent one of the qualities of really bad playwriting.

Then the other man arrives. He has been delayed by having to call on a lady whose son has made an outrageous misalliance. He tells of this, and of the expected result of the marriage—that the man will be ostracized by society. Tanqueray hears part of this, returns to his letters, and this time apparently hears more. It stops his being able to write, and he goes into another room to finish. Then we learn about his past, and his dead wife, the first Mrs. Tanqueray. When he returns, the two other men leave, and the play really starts, with Tanqueray and his best friend settling down, and the release of the news that the Second Mrs. Tanqueray is a lady with the same kind of past as the one previously discussed.

Now this kind of thing will not be accepted in the theater today. It was accepted very well when the play was first produced in 1893 (though Bernard Shaw—an Ibsenite—was distressed by it), and William Archer in his book on *Play-making* (published in 1912) defends it almost *in toto*. But it gets weaker as the years go by. Each time an audience sees something of that kind, it becomes more and more aware of its faults.

I should, perhaps, take a few moments to analyze what those faults are. First, they are the appearance of two characters who are never seen again. They are not characters, they are puppets needed to establish certain information. This is something that all authors should watch out for. I have done it, myself, and I know. In *Diversion* I used in the first act a young woman who was never seen again. She put over certain information that could have just as easily been handled by someone else, and I made a weak attempt to justify her presence by making her the sister of the young man (also never seen) whom the daughter later married. This did not do any good. The character should never have been there at all.

Second, there are Aubrey's notes. If we ever knew what these were, if they were important to the plot, if they achieved anything that helped the play to move, they would be less offensive. But even then it is doubtful whether a host would write them in such circumstances, or whether his guests would start talking about him while he was in the room. The room is not so divided that conversation cannot be heard from one end to the other. Cayley's conversation drives Aubrey from the room five minutes later.

Third, Cayley's description of the first Mrs. Tanqueray seems dragged in. The men, old friends of Aubrey's, know nothing about her. Their only contributions to the conversation are remarks like "Abroad, you mean?" "Miscalculated?" and "Didn't that—?" The scene is merely to tell the audience. It is only after they have left, and the question of their all going out somewhere together has been almost wholly forgotten, that we get down to a scene we can recognize as having some relation, not, I would say, to real life (where anything can happen, and all sorts of characters never appear again), but to what we have now come to accept as a true stage representation of life.

What we have so come to accept changes, as I have said, from year to year. We like to think of it as getting better, surer, more efficient, less obvious. One of our troubles is that it has got so much better that we have grown a little bored with it, that having learned to know and recognize a "well-made play," we no longer care too much about it. There are scenes in plays which would, normally, not have taken place where the author has set them. They would have taken place in another room, and the playwright has been put to some trouble to find reasons why they take place where they would not. (The other room is being cleaned, the fire smokes, the ceiling is leaking; these are the more obvious devices.) Occasionally, he does not bother to explain at all. It is simpler just to go ahead and play the scenes where he wants them. Lillian Hellman gave this explanation for having the good-byes to the children in *Watch on the Rhine* take place in the downstairs living room, when quite obviously the father would have gone upstairs to the children. It seemed to her like too much technical trouble to avoid a very small jolt. I can deeply sympathize with her on this point, but I am not sure that, even so, I would advise other playwrights to follow her example, unless the whole play was constructed in defiance of the "well-made" technique.

We have come, as I have said, slightly to despise the well-made play, which was once the darling of the theater. Clifford Bax, in his book, has said: "We ought to admire the well-made play as we admire a well-made man, and if we were to elaborate this analogy we should find that many modern plays are skinny creatures or cripples or over-large in the head." I agree with this, but I also want, nowadays, to be sure that the well-made play is something more than just that. We have all of us met plenty of well-made men who had nothing in their heads at all. Brains are what count, both places. Too much well-madeness can empty a play considerably. I think that, too, is what Lillian Hellman had in mind. The balance must lie somewhere in between, unless one is going to write a new kind of play.

The move toward this has already started. It has been re-ported to me that Arthur Miller, when asked why he wrote

Death of a Salesman with such an odd and time-jumping construction, explained that to construct a well-made play (as he
had already proved that he could do with *All My Sons*) meant
wasting time in writing scenes that were of little interest to the
author, and therefore presumably to the audience, scenes that
joined other scenes, scenes that gave time for things to happen,
scenes that—according to the deepest vitality of the play—were
almost like padding scenes. He preferred to concentrate on
scenes that were of the true essence of what he was writing
about, to isolate that essence and confine himself to it. I think
that the better and newer plays are trying to do this. Much of the
old padding has disappeared from them. The number of characters is diminishing. The plot-line is simpler, clearer. The
mood and the basic emotional quality of the play are more
closely adhered to. This is perhaps the beginning of a new kind
of drama. Its rules are not yet formed. They depend on the
depth and inner sincerity of the author's intention. I am inclined
to think that an acquaintance with the older rules of the well-
made play is still a good basis for learning how to break them. I
would also like to add that I am all for seeing them broken.

CHAPTER SIX

The Unities

WE HAVE landed ourselves now into the problem of our opening, and the information of the audience of things that it has to know, without its being apparent that it is being so informed. This starts a further investigation. How much stuff can have happened before the play begins, and how much must be shown happening?

One of Ibsen's great contributions to the theater was to try to make almost everything have happened before the play opened, to start his play where almost all playwrights would formerly have ended it. In this way, an enormous amount of time is saved, and a greater portion of the play is a passionate analysis of the past. The audiences now will not feel that they are being told things merely in order to set the play going; they will not get impatient with the exposition, because they will know that it is not exposition, but the play itself, and they will be caught up with it. This is truer of Ibsen's later plays. The early scene in *A Doll's House* where Nora tells Mrs. Linden a great deal of the preceding plot is still not too unlike a technical piece of stage confidence to the friend who has just returned from a long absence, and has therefore to be told everything that has happened while he was away. This character is to be avoided. It is too obviously there for just that purpose.

Other playwrights feel that as much should happen on stage as possible. This is wise, provided that what happens on stage is vital and necessary to what the play is about. Merely preliminary scenes, landing the characters where the true action can begin, are a bore and a bother, and they take too long. Prologues, too, can give the impression of being tied to the play with Scotch tape. Yet information has to be put over. The skill with which it is done is part of what goes to make the well-made play. In older plays the characters were in the habit of telling their past history in soliloquy to the audience. This was rebelled at, with all the ensuing devices of servants discussing their master's business and past, and the kind of opening that even Ibsen devised for *The Wild Duck*, where an off-stage party is being watched, described and accounted for. The methods grew more subtle, less noticeable, and then, of recent years, the older device has started to creep back, largely through the introduction of a figure called "The Narrator," who may even be one of the principal characters himself. I have used this figure more than once. In *I Remember Mama* and in *I Am a Camera*, a leading character (a writer, in each case) has an opening soliloquy, in which a number of facts are put across, with no effort made to let the exposition seem natural or lifelike. I cannot express the relief and pleasure of being able to do this. But once used, once the device has been settled on, it must be used again. It must be made a part of the play. A slightly new technique has been employed, and the audience must be shown, as fast as possible, how it is to be managed. It must be shown what it is to expect. Tennessee Williams did it, too, in *The Glass Menagerie,* and James Bridie in *The Black Eye.* In those two plays, the narrator acknowledges the audience and the fact that he is addressing them, as did the Stage Manager in *Our Town.* In the two plays of my own, he does not; he is a writer, talking aloud to himself. Perhaps audiences are more willing to allow that to writers.

From these signs we may go a long way; actually, a long way backward. We may get letters read aloud by their recipients again, and we may get back to the aside. Eugene O'Neill used it in *Strange Interlude* and, in another way, in *The Great God Brown.* I was impatient with the device then, seeing it as a method by which the playwright shirked his job. But a number of years have passed now, and I am not under the influence of Ibsen as rigidly as I then was. Now I am not so sure of my displeasure. But as with drawing, and with the laws of harmony, it is essential first to know what the rules are, to be able to submit to them, and then deliberately to set out to refute them. I do not regret the years spent in learning how to handle exposition in the conventional way, and in trying to do it more simply and less obviously every time.

Quite apart from Ibsen, there are many reasons for starting the story as far on in itself as is possible. One of them is that there is never much time in the theater, and what there is seems to be getting less every year. The curtain rises later, and the audiences cannot be kept in their seats after eleven o'clock. This is the answer of most managements to whom one must submit

oneself. Now and then, as in *The King and I,* the time is
stretched, sometimes by almost forty-five minutes. The reply to
trying to make that a general rule is, in that case, that the show
is a musical. I cannot really see the difference. If the show is interesting, I think the audience will stay to see it out, and that
otherwise it will not. But custom rules here. With the shortening
of time, the author needs all that he can get to tell what is truthfully his story, and must not waste any of it on preliminaries. At
least, this makes for a tighter and better kind of playwriting.

When I was starting to plan *The Damask Cheek* this exact
problem presented itself. Since the play dealt with the ad-
ventures of an English girl in America, it seemed right to start
it with her arrival at the home of her New York relatives. It
would provide an opportunity to portray the details of such an
arrival on the stage. It reminded me a little of the first act of
The Cherry Orchard, with the return of Madame Ranevsky,
which had always enchanted me. I had long wanted to draw
such an arrival on the stage, remembering the annual or biennial
arrivals at my home in London, when I was a child, of my rich
and attractive aunt who lived in New York. I could remember
myself running out into the street, looking up and down the
roads for the taxi (or was it still a four-wheeler?) driving her
from the station to our home. I had sketched such an arrival in
The Distaff Side, but on a smaller scale, and *The Damask Cheek*
gave every opportunity to do it properly. The act was very
largely planned already. I had arranged which members of the
family had gone to meet the boat, and which had stayed at
home. I had invented all the domestic fuss in the household,
and the conversations of the children, which would reveal the
things needed to be known about the heroine. Then she would

arrive. More talk, more confidences, more details of a far too elaborately invented family, plans for the dance that was to be given for her, discreet questions as to why she was not yet married, scenes between her and the children. It was all delightful. Act Two was to be the dance.

But as I came to consider it (and thank goodness, I had not yet started to write the play), I knew that something was wrong. The whole first act was preparation, and only preparation. The play would not, could not, really start until the day of the dance. The dance typified everything, gave birth to all the slender action. The wait between Acts One and Two would be a dead wait (I had almost written "weight"), because nothing had been set in motion. Since nothing started until the day of the dance, I realized that the only thing to do was to open the play on that day. The heroine would have arrived about ten days earlier: she could have got to know her American family, and now could talk to them, herself. The details of her actual arrival, attractive as they seemed to me to portray, would have to be left out. This is one of the penalties of playwriting. You cannot have all of the fun, all of the time.

Also, the story, slight as it was, would have begun. Something would be under way—the forthcoming dance, the preparations for the evening, the people who had been invited, and the prospect of what it all might bring forth. It is a good thing for something to have happened before the curtain rises, not to catch the characters at a total ebb of action, but to find them when something, in some way relevant to what the play is to be about, has started to move. They are not then stuck in flat conversation about nothing. We see them at work in a situation. What this situation is to be has to be carefully considered. I made a mistake in this regard, once. In *Behold We Live,* the curtain rose on a highly dramatic scene. The late Miss Gertrude Lawrence, in evening dress, was seated in an armchair, and her husband was pointing a revolver at her, threatening to shoot her. I was proud of myself for thinking of that opening. It was a bad one. In the first place, since Miss Lawrence was the star, the audience knew perfectly well that the shot would not be fired, as the program gave no hint that the remainder of the play was to be a flash-back. Secondly, and this is more important, I had started the play at far too high a pitch. I had to come down from it, and was never able to reach as high again. It was written for two reasons. First, I had known of a marriage where that was quite a usual thing, and the husband was given to indulging in scenes of that kind. That was all very well, but it still gave me nowhere to progress to. Secondly, I had remembered the opening of Maurine Watkins' *Chicago,* where the curtain rose on the leading lady firing a pistol into a man's body, and screaming words of abuse at him as he fell to the floor. That was an excellent opening. The play was about her trial for the murder, and the fake characterizations of sympathy and innocence that were put on her for the jury and the public. It was essential that we should see her, for one swift, blinding moment, as she really was. The opening of *Chicago* was in key with the remainder of the play. The opening of *Behold We Live* was not. The opening of *The Damask Cheek* that I had planned was in key, but it led nowhere. These things I now know. I know that they have something to do with those mysterious powers called the Unities.

I must take a little time on the Unities. One does not hear of them as much now as one used to, but they are there, like the statues of forbidding gods in the background. What their powers are, no one is quite sure of. What are those three Unities of Action, Time and Space? They come, I believe, from Aristotle, whom I have never read. I have long been under the impression that they meant that the play should be all on one note, with every incident conducive to maintaining that note, and all in one set and without any time interruption. The Greek tragedies all seem to follow that ruling. How essential was it in modern drama to follow them? Most modern plays did not, I knew. Why, then, do people go on about them, still?

There is an incident in *Nicholas Nickleby* (which contains more good stuff about the theater than any other novel of my acquaintance) where Nicholas and the actress, Miss Snevellicci, go to call on a Mr. Curdle to ask him to become a patron of Miss Snevellicci's "bespeak." Mr. Curdle, who will reappear in these pages later, is a patron of the Drama. He is the kind of gentleman, living in a provincial town, whom we all know extremely well today. He is effulgent and literary, he has a tremendous memory, and he talks highfalutin nonsense, to which we, when we visit his house as we always have to do, are obliged to listen politely. He always deplores the present state of the theater. So did Mr. Curdle. "As an exquisite embodiment of the poet's visions, and a realization of human intellectuality," he declaims, "gilding with refulgent light our dreamy moments, and laying open a new and magic world before the mental eye, the drama is gone, perfectly gone." One longs to ask him what plays he was thinking of. The trouble is that they would be impossible to find, any longer, if there were any.

To Mr. Curdle, Nicholas, a new young playwright, is introduced. He speaks of his new play, and Mr. Curdle asks whether

he has observed the Unities. Nicholas, as I would have liked to
do, asks what the Unities are.

Mr. Curdle coughed and considered. "The Unities, sir," he said,
"are a completeness—a kind of universal dove-tailedness with
regard to place and time—a sort of general oneness, if I may be
allowed to use so strong an expression. I take these to be the dramatic unities, so far as I have been enabled to bestow attention upon
them, and I have read much upon the subject, and thought much. I
find, running through the performances of this child," [here he
turned to that fascinating and grisly figure known as the Infant
Phenomenon] "a unity of feeling, a breadth, a light and shade, a
warmth of coloring, a tone, a harmony, a glow, an artistical development of original conceptions, which I look for in vain among
older performers. That is my definition of the Unities of Drama."

One has heard and read many speeches like that in life; there
are modern drama critics who write in exactly that way. And
yet, despite the fun that can be made of the Unities, there is a
good deal to be said for them and for the "sort of general oneness, if I may be allowed to use so strong an expression."

Let us look at the Unities again. The joining of the first act
of *The Damask Cheek* to the others, by making the dance the
general unifier, helped to prove the Unity of Action to me. We
are all aware of a need for a oneness of mood, and will seldom
try and swing from comedy to tragedy in the same play. It is
hard to ask the audience to make that switch, too. It can be
done. It was done superbly by Sean O'Casey in *Juno and the
Paycock,* and also in *The Plough and the Stars.* These two plays
swung from broad farce to intensest tragic emotion, sometimes
in a quarter of a page, and without warning. The setting helped
that, with the mood of Ireland in the time of the troubles, and the
characters helped it, too, as did the opening lines which set the

note for tragedy to come, but the comic scenes were so broad that only a genius, possessed of a deep poetic instinct, could have managed it. It is safer to know where you stand and to stay there, letting the audience know it, too. It is more likely to stay there with you.

This attention of the audience is the most important thing that a playwright has to remember. He must never let that attention flag or wander away from him. His job is to carry it along, and to do nothing that will jolt it out of forgetting that it is in a theater. The audience is there to pretend, to pretend that what is going on is real. It knows perfectly well that it is not real, but it will do its best to forget that while the play is happening. How else could it ever cry? You must not remind it in any way that the whole thing is a game, unless you make a condition, apparent from the moment that your play starts, that that is the kind of entertainment it is going to see. An audience is like a group of children. Rupert Brooke, in his book on Webster, compared it to children who are perfectly prepared to play any game of pretense, so long as its terms were made clear to them. "Let us," says Uncle George, "pretend that she is a hen, and he is a steam-roller, and I am an angry cow." That is fine, and the children will stay within the frame. But let Uncle George forget the cow role for a moment, let him return to being Uncle George, and the children become furious.

Having been long ago trained as a lawyer, I have often thought of the theater as being a bargain between audience and author, and of the program as being the contract of that bargain, or the evidence of it. Its terms are simple. "The audience will pretend that the play is real, and the author will do everything in his power to assist it in that pretense." The things he does, the skill he employs in doing them, are what are called his construction and his technique. The Unities are there to help those.

The Unity of Place involves the changing of sets. As seldom as possible, would be my motto. There are several reasons for this, of which the modern cost of scene-changing, as well as of building and designing them, is only one. Staying in one set helps to sustain the mood, and to keep the audience within it. Suppose, for example, you have a play idea which depends on the longing of a prisoner-of-war to return to his home and his family, and the fulfillment of that longing, the things he finds when he comes home. The first impulse will be to set the first act in the prison camp, and to show that longing visually to the audience, to show the hero in his daydreams, and all the plans he has made for the day when he is returned. Now, think for a moment what that will mean. It will mean establishing the camp on the stage, the boredom, the humiliation, the endless routine. It will mean showing the guards and the enemy, it will mean drawing other men in the camp, setting up those brief friendships that such an existence can bring. It can be done quite easily, but it will take time. A third of the play will be gone by the time it has been done. Then you will have to go home, create the home as the camp was created, and with the home, the family and the stories that have come into being while the hero was away. That will take time, too. And then, and only then, will the play start. All the rest was preparation. And the other characters, the men in the camp, the guards and the leaders of the enemy, what will happen to them? They will have disappeared, never to be used again. Was it worth while to have created them? And where, quite simply, is the general oneness? Where is the audience's attention to be directed? If it likes and was interested in the prison camp, it will resent being asked to focus that attention now on the home life.

How this story can be better told is another thing. I would suggest setting it all in the home, focusing on the home. The hero's letters can be quoted before his arrival, telling of his longing to return. Or the play can start with his arrival when everyone is out, if such a thing can happen. Then he can talk to the cook, or to his child, if one has been left around, or to his pal whom he has brought with him. His dreams can be put over in that way. There are many other methods, but the one thing I feel sure of is that a whole act should not be devoted to preparation. And the first thing to find out is how much is preparation, and how much is a part of the play. Far more of any story is preparation than one is likely at first to realize.

Am I recommending that every play should be set in one place only? I am not. I think it is a good thing if it can be done, but it cannot always be done. Then the scene must be changed, and as often as need be, trying one's hardest not to need to. Audiences do not like plays in one set, I have often been told. They get bored looking at it. That may be true, but I can think of a great many that they have liked. It is like telling me that they like to see the leading lady in a different dress every time she appears. I know that audiences appreciate changes of scene and of costume, but I know, too, that they must not be given in to too far. I have seen plays where the leading lady (perhaps a movie actress) wore a succession of gowns which elicited a series of "oh's" and "ah's" from the female members of the audience, but the plays were not successes for that reason. They were very often not successful at all. The "oh's" and "ah's" are very nice, they can help to charm an author's or producer's heart, but the play must come first. The audience's attention must come first.

Changing sets will deflect that attention when it is wasteful or unnecessary. Then the audience becomes aware that it is in a theater again, aware of the waits, and it becomes restless, starting to fidget and to chatter. I am against plays with too many scenes, for the same reason, unless the changes can be made instantly, as they were in *I Remember Mama.* I am against plays which change the whole locale, moving from the country to the city, from the occident to the orient, and changing the majority of the characters as well. The audience has got used to the place, to the type of life and the people that have been put before it, and will not like having to get to know a whole new set of these. There are a dozen further developments of this theory.

Lastly, there is the Unity of Time. Many of the same reasons operate here. Great gaps of time are hard for the audience to assimilate. It obviously is no longer essential that the whole action of a play should be continuous, but time-lapses need a little consideration. I have certain personal predilections on the subject, though I am not sure that they are more than that. I have a certain sense of shape, and I like the time divisions to be more or less equal. I do not care to have a single day's division between Acts One and Two, and a ten-year interval between Acts Two and Three. It spoils a pattern, though I may be more sensitive to pattern than is necessary. It is not always possible to follow my sense of it. I greatly disliked having a two-month interval between the last two scenes of the third act of *Bell, Book and Candle,* but I could see no way to manage without it. No one has complained of it. I like the divisions to be tidy, and to feel a shapeliness about the play. If there is a scene division in the first act, I prefer to have it again during the evening, preferably in the last act. A setup that I am fond of is a first act in two scenes, a second act in one scene, and a third act in two scenes, divided as Act One was divided. That is shapely. A three-act play with no scene divisions, all in the same set, and with not more than a few hours between the acts, is the tidiest of all. I always feel a rather childlike pride when I have managed to write a whole act without a scene division, and a longing hope that I will be able to keep it up for the rest of the play. I seldom can.

How many acts? Not more than three, we all now know. That is of recent development. Plays used to be in four or even five acts. The last act was usually a feeble little one, winding everything up. One of the worst of all last acts, from this point of view, is in Clyde Fitch's *Woman in the Case*. The play is over at the end of Act Three, which finishes on a good, screaming, headbanging scene between two women. The reaction of the audience who had had to sit and wait (smoking was not common, then) and listen to entr'acte music until the final ten-minute reconciliation between husband and wife was tepidly staged, must have been an irritable one. Perhaps that is one of the reasons why the weak last act generally disappeared. Two-act plays are growing more and more popular. I, myself, like them very much. But they must be conceived as being in two acts from the start. There will be no more beginning, middle and end. There will be a halfway mark in the story, that is all. It is a good device, because it prevents the audience's attention from being broken more than once. Once, apparently, is essential. You cannot do a play in one act. If you try to, someone will break it up for you. But the two-act play is gaining ground. I suspect it will become the popular thing before too long has gone by. When four- or five-act plays are revived now, the divisions are made to put them into two or three. These divisions are not always successful. The author knew what he was doing when he constructed the play, and his stresses are placed for his own intermissions. The divisions may well happen in the wrong place. That is unfortunate.

And while we are on the subject of time, the prologue, epilogue and flash-back can be considered. These are all tempting, and they are all dangerous. They are sometimes essential. A prologue and epilogue are necessary when the play is seen at a distance, and when the irony of time is involved as an active ingredient. They can set off the tale, explain why it is being told, point its moral, and show what happened to the characters years later and how they felt about it all, then. The flash-back is really the whole play, if it is long enough, with the other acts as lengthy prologues and epilogues, or it is a kind of prologue, itself, set in the middle, to explain things. I have used all of these. In a play called *Somebody Knows* I used the prologue and epilogue. I was not satisfied with the ones that were played, and I rewrote them for the published amateur acting edition. I am still not wholly satisfied. I thought they were necessary—I still think so —because the play was the story of an unsolved murder, and I wanted it to be seen as we see such stories when we read of them, afterward, in books of crime. I used the flash-back in *Flowers of the Forest,* taking the characters back to World War I. The war period was an essential part of my play, and I needed a memory of it as the maturer characters looked back on it, having half-remembered and half-forgotten it.

Paul Osborn has used the flash-back in his dramatization of *Point of No Return.* It was made essential by the story that he was adapting. The hero is seen to go back home and be rejected in his youth by the girl he seriously loved. It is unfortunate that we know, from the first act, that he no longer loves her now, being happily married to someone else. The rejection makes little or no difference, no serious or permanent stamp on his character when we see it. This tends to keep the audience away from the story, stops its being involved with it. There is the last and final test, whether or not you have claimed its attention. If you have, anything is permissible, and the Unities go down with a collapsing bang. It is up to you to know whether you have or not.

CHAPTER SEVEN

The Set, the Start and the People

Y OU ARE about to write the words "Act One" on paper. It is a quite exciting moment. It is the moment when your play is starting. It is the rise of the curtain, when the lights in the front of the house have dimmed down, and there is a new and awaiting silence in the audience. And because of the excitement of that moment, there is also a quality of fear in it. I am always scared to start on a new play, look for and find excuses to delay the writing of those words. This is true of my approach to work at any time, a strange mixture of intense desire and reluctance that makes me do anything, anything down to filing my finger nails, rather than take the initial step on the typewriter. "Filing my nails" has become a stock phrase for the deliberate delay in starting work with me. When I began *Young Woodley*, my first successful play, I had everything prepared to start work right after lunch. I delayed by buying rulers, erasers, red ink, making up the sheets, so that it was not until after dinner that I forced myself to those first words. In the end you will have to write them, and actually there is nothing that you want more to do. Stop filing your nails, and begin. State your scene, and the time of day that it takes place. How much else should you describe, how much detail of the set should you go into?

Up till now, I have been gentle in my admonitions. I have hinted and suggested, and in the end I have left it all to you. In this case, I will not. I will speak my mind, and squarely. Put in just as little as you can. State the type of room, or exterior, state how many doors you think you will need (you will still quite often be wrong), any absolutely essential pieces of furniture (like the stove in *Hedda Gabler,* and that would presumably be essential in any Norwegian house and need not, therefore, be mentioned either), and let it go at that. "The drawing room of a Park Avenue apartment," "The kitchen of a farmhouse in the Middle West"; these are, to me, the ideal stage directions.

I know all about Shaw's stage directions, and Granville Barker's, with their long essays on current conditions and on all the pasts of their characters, and the J. M. Barrie ones, too, with their winsome and tricky little remarks about: "Watch that screen. It is bound to be used later on." I still say, do not copy them. From the best playwrights, they are an irritation. From any but the best, they are maddening. They can quite easily stop the play from being read. Once you are a success, you can put them into the printed edition, if you must, but wait until then. Producers, agents, directors will not read stage directions, any stage directions. There was a famous director who confessed to it. A playwright of my acquaintance asked him what would happen if an author were to write a stage direction in which a character took out a revolver and shot another character, without a word of dialogue to explain it. The director replied that he would merely go on wondering why that character had ceased to talk. That may be an exaggeration, but remember it. The producer and director want to get to the play, and to let it tell them everything they need to know.

The same thing applies to descriptions of the characters. Please do not include them, or any comments on their personalities. The directions to the effect that "Lydia is a frank and charming girl at first sight. We shall see later that she has a fiercely jealous disposition, which can perhaps be noted in the curl of her lip, the gesture with which she empties the trash basket"—these are all in the wrong place. They belong to novels. They belong in your dialogue. They belong to your director. Leave them all out. Tell us how old Lydia is, whether she is good-looking or not, and let it go at that. Do not even tell us if she is a blonde or a brunette, unless it is essential to the plot. That can hinder your casting. The longer you write, the briefer you will try and make your stage directions. I was tempted by the personal and intimate ones myself in my earlier days. I loved the J. M. Barrie descriptions, and set myself out to copy them. I remember starting one play (it was never finished) with a stage direction which began: "The audience—assuming we are lucky enough to have one—is seated under the cedar tree facing the Johnsons' house." Do I have to comment on that any further?

Do not try to design the sets. You will not be able to help trying to do so, and you will find that the designer will undo it all. I have sometimes thought that designers quite deliberately try to switch the doors and the windows from the side where the author placed them to the other side of the stage, and for no reason other than to be difficult. This has happened to me with almost every play that I have written. But, mainly, the designer can do a better job on it than you can, just as you can write a better script than he could. It is your business. Indicate what you need or think that you must have, and be prepared to see it all changed. This is especially so if you are going in for one of the more modern and complicated sets, one of the skeleton sets, showing several rooms at a time. You will have ideas as to how this is to be managed, but the designer will have better ones. Trust him. The elaborate settings for *I Remember Mama* were the designer's idea. I knew what I wanted, I knew what I needed to show, but I did not know how it was to be managed. The small revolving stages were the designer's idea, as were the steps up to the main stage. Now, when the play is done by amateurs, other and simpler devices are used. Leave it to the director and designer.

You will tell me that you have to be able to visualize it all in your head, that you must be able to see it all as happening while you write it. That is quite true. See it, visualize it all you can, but do not try to force it onto paper as a kind of "must." Actually, you will not be able to see it all happening, moving from scene to scene. An odd thing will occur. You will have visualized the sofa in a certain position, you will see the first scenes being played from it where it is. Then, later on, and you will never know when or how this happened, you will write another scene played on the sofa, and you will have seen it in a different place. You will not be aware of this until the play comes to be produced, and then the move from the sofa to the door will not work out, because one or the other has changed its position. Very few authors can keep sufficient detachment from their plays to see them acted all the time.

The same suggestion should operate on all the ensuing stage directions. Make them as few as possible. Do not take up time with the small details of stage business that have occurred to you. I am reminded of my own first play about *Mary, Queen of Scots* here. The last act of that play was set in Fotheringay Castle on the morning of Mary's execution, and I opened it with two servants announcing what was going to happen—presumably, if I know anything about young playwrights, in one line. And then there was a stage direction: "She drapes a picture in black." It was that line that so amused my mother. I am still not quite sure why. Perhaps it was the inadequacy of one small detail to represent the whole, which has now a vague relation to expressionism in the theater. Perhaps it was a resemblance to the hanging of one last ornament on an already decorated Christmas tree. I was reminded of it in reading George Kelly's play, *Daisy Mayme,* where a character enters "Eating an After Dinner Mint." I laughed at that piece of business as my mother had laughed at mine. I still do not know quite why. Perhaps I saw "One After Dinner Mint" on the stage manager's list of hand-props. Perhaps it was the excessive detail of the direction. I think I know why Kelly inserted it—and after all, he is his own director—but I still doubt if he was wise. Keep the directions down until rehearsal. Then you can tell them, privately, to the director.

Your initial stage description, as simple as possible, is written. Now come your characters. How do you start? Should the leading man or woman be on the stage when the curtain rises, or not? Once, the answer would firmly have been "No." A star, in those days, demanded an entrance, and an entrance had to be worked up. The character was talked about, described, praised, waited for until the exactly right moment had arrived for his entrance. That, I thank God, is a thing of the past. There is no reason why a star should not be discovered at the rise of the curtain. In most of my plays, they have been. What about the audience, and the habit of late arrival? Can you start the play instantaneously at the curtain rise? Will the audience be able to hear those first words in all the shuffling and seat-banging that goes on? Here, I think, a concession can and should be made. That shuffling and seat-banging will happen at the start of each act. The opening lines will be muffled, sometimes missed. I think the author should remember this. I think he should—not waste his first few moments, but do his best to fill them with things that are valuable, but not essential; the absence of hearing which will not make nonsense of the play. That is another reason why the first few minutes of a play are such a trial to the author. I have never started a script without the certainty that those first three pages at least would have to be rewritten later on. Actually, they never have been, though they have usually had to be cut. But that is one of my faults.

How fast can one go in the opening? The proper answer is "as fast as you can," and that is usually not fast enough. I, myself, have a tendency to start very slowly. I want to elaborate, to build my characters, to establish everything that I can. It would seem that I can never trust my audience sufficiently. The first ten or fifteen minutes of my plays lag and linger. There is an advantage to this in the fact that when I do start, when the action gets itself under way, the audience knows everything that I want it to about my people. It is interested in them, it will follow their movements, and it might well not have done that if I had taken less time to prepare my stage. That, at least, is what I tell myself, but I know, too, that my openings are not as good as I would like them to be.

There is the business of establishing atmosphere, especially the atmosphere of anywhere new or special. You set your play backstage at a circus, in a lawyer's office, in the stockroom of a large department store, and you feel that you must establish the atmosphere of the background before you start the story. That is not true. The atmosphere must be established, but it should be done simultaneously with other things. The attention of the audience toward incidents directly connected with the play must be the first consideration, and the atmosphere should be worked in with that. Ten minutes of atmosphere and then start the story, is more likely to be my own rule. I am not defending this. It is part of my distaste for plot, and for having to start one. A play that was all atmosphere, with no plot at all, would be my preference; in any case, the smallest modicum of plot that can be thrown in to hold the play together. That was what I did in my play, *London Wall*, which has not been seen in America. It was a play set in a London lawyer's office, a background which I knew extremely well. All the detail of the office, the lives and conversations of the typists and the male clerks are extremely well done. They take up a good deal more than half of the play. The remainder is a Cinderella story that is almost shamelessly inadequate. That is why the play has never been played over here. The detail of the office is too unfamiliar to American audiences, using and capitalizing on temporary clichés of phraseology, details of places and pastimes which were instantly identifiable, and with pleasure, to London audiences. To a New York audience they would mean nothing, and the weakness of the story would be twice as apparent.

Do not be dilatory, as I am. Embark on that opening situation, however small, that has the characters already at work. Look at the opening of J. M. Barrie's play, *What Every Woman*

Knows, and the speed with which the basic situation of Maggie Wylie with her empty and longing heart is started. One of her brothers, set as a comedy character in the opening lines in which he speaks of love, asking what his brothers think he would do with such a thing, remarks: "Though Maggie is undersized, she has a passion for romance." This is an admirable opening to one of the best first acts ever written. It obeys everything. It sets the comedy key, it sets up Maggie's past with the mention of the Minister she was hoping for, who has now announced his betrothal to someone else, and it perfectly fills up those difficult first few minutes. If these things are not heard, the play will not be ruined. What is essential is the incident of the burglars who have been visiting the house. The mention of them is delayed until page four, but no time has been wasted. The dialogue has humor and characterization, and it gives us information. "Though Maggie is undersized, she has a passion for romance." The plain young woman who longs for love is a dangerous figure, she could be an unattractive one. The word "undersized" is perfect here; it, and the deep affection her brothers have for her, remove a great deal of the danger. "It's ill done of the Minister," says the brother. "Many a pound of steak has that man had in this house." Here is comedy again.

The openings of all Barrie's plays are good. *Dear Brutus* opens with the ladies of a house party concocting a telegram to the police, denouncing the butler for having stolen their jewelry. They hand the telegram to him to dispatch, forcing him to read it aloud, and then they promise not to send it if he will tell them what they most want to know—why they have all been invited to this strange week end. It is well imagined, better contrived, with the formal return of the stolen rings on a salver to each lady, and the whole revealing dialogue, not only of situation, but also of character. *Mary Rose* has a superb and chilling opening, which sets the stage for a mood of eeriness that is part of the evening. And *Alice Sit-by-the-fire* has the best opening line that I can remember in any play. A boy and girl of thirteen and fourteen are seated together. The boy is reading a telegram, and then he says—it is the first line in the play: "All I can say is that if father tries to kiss me, I shall kick him."

There is a tremendous amount to be learned from Barrie. It has become the fashion to make fun of him, to laugh at his sentiment (and a good deal of it is hard to take nowadays), but technically he was amazing. His effects are those of a truly fine conjurer. You cannot see him achieving them. The only trouble is that they are so seldom copyable, because they seem to be wholly individual to his especial scene or need of the moment, as well as to his own odd personality. They have not the worthy solidity of Ibsen's, where the rule appears to be as rigid as that of any puritan father—no character shall make an entrance or an exit that does not also further the plot and purpose of the play, and there shall be no detail or incident that does not do the same thing. One admires those rulings, one despairs of ever being able to follow them. Barrie's technique is trickier, more flashy, more elusive. It reminds one very slightly of that of Sacha Guitry, who never stopped employing all the details of the stage and its devices so that they seemed to glitter and to tinkle like glass chandeliers. It is wholly personal. It is admirable. It is never wholly realistic; it is always just off center, but it can start a ball rolling in one's head, even if it be only the ball of how never to use the easy and obvious way of doing anything.

I shall return to Barrie again when I am dealing with the

mechanisms of technique. For the moment, I should return to those characters who are waiting for their first lines. The theater has grown up enough by now for your no longer having to start with your lesser people and then work up to your leads. There should, in the first place, be as few lesser people as possible. You will try not to open your play as did Sir Arthur Pinero in *His House in Order* with the hero's secretary being interviewed by a journalist so that the relevant facts to his marriages may be revealed. Neither secretary nor journalist is used again, neither is a character, they are only dummies. One had rather the stage manager came forward and told you what you were supposed to know, or that it had been printed on the program like the "New Readers Begin Here" passage that preludes serial stories in the magazines.

There are no rules, naturally, as to how many characters you should have. I have used as few as three, and as many as twenty-two. I prefer to use as few as possible, if only for the fact that the longer one has with a character, the better one is able to descend into and analyze him. The more characters one has, the quicker one will have to be in establishing them. At the dress rehearsal of *The Distaff Side* in London, we played a version in which the third of the sisters, the lesser of the three, drawn from the aunt who had told me the initial incident, made her entrance with other characters in an ensemble scene in the second act. Marc Connelly was at the rehearsal, and he came to me with the complaint that it took him too long to realize who she was, and what kind of a person. Her first lines were thrown into a group scene, and she remained vague and unclear until her own big scene later on. To remedy this, I wrote her in an earlier entrance, which did nothing but establish—and speedily—her character. And it was then that my subconscious, thoroughly approving of what I was doing, it would seem, handed me an excellent line—the character's own first line in the play. Cocktails, dry Martinis, are being served. The young girl offers her one. "I don't think I will, dear," is her reply. "I'll have the cherry, if there is one."

That line did the trick. It established Nellie as I wanted her— her general unfamiliarity with cocktails, and her assumption that they always contained cherries. She had a later line which always got a much larger laugh than I would have anticipated. She asks after the young man who has just left the stage, and is told that he is the son of a famous playwright. "Oh, I wish I'd known," she says. "I'd have had a better look at him." I can only assume the size of the laugh to have been due to a total identification with her of all the women in the audience, who knew that it was what they themselves would have thought, if not said, in a similar circumstance.

The young man who had just left the stage was one of the dummy characters, one of the bad dummies. He is better than the girl in *Diversion* because he appears in the second act as well as the first, and he is part of the plot. He is the rich and successful young man whom the heroine thinks she wants to marry; he provides the conflict with the young man, poor but promising, whom she does ultimately marry. He could perfectly well have been a part, a fully conceived character. Why isn't he? I can only suppose because I was not really interested in him, or his section of the story. I said earlier that the plot of the young girl sufficed to make a basis or peg on which to hang the play and all the things I wanted to say about women. I said that "sufficed" was the right word. It was. The young girl's story will just do. The girl herself, and her poorer boy-friend will just do, because I had conceived them as people. I had given them a sex relationship, and I had let them have doubts about it, about the rightness of it, and of their basic attitude toward each other. In expressing those doubts, they became human beings. But the other young man was a device to help another device. I did not bother with him at all. He was a young man who made his first appearance wearing a white tie, and a white tie would have done almost as well as an actor to play him. "Enter a White Tie" could have been his stage direction. He entered, he spoke, he made sense, he even got a laugh or two, but he did not happen. I was not interested. I just believed in him, and that was all. It is not enough. You must do more than believe in your characters, they must also be able to surprise you. You must learn things about them, as you go along. If you do not, if they merely progress as you knew they would, say the right and correct things only, then you are in danger.

You are in danger, because they will emerge as dummies. This is what happens to the fill-in characters, the guests at house parties who are there merely because, since there is a house party, there must be guests at it. There have been quite a few of these, even in the better comedies, and they have always been deadly. There are characters, of course, who cannot help being dummies, who should be dummies. These are the messengers, the maids who bring in the tea or the cocktail things and announce visitors, or the grocery boy who delivers the supplies. It has been recommended that even these should not be dummies, and that the good playwright can always characterize them, give them a touch of reality and personality, as the actor is always supposed to find a chance to do the same thing. I am by no means sure about this. Too often, if the playwright tries to do that, he will be forcing an issue and wasting time, time that he needs for other things, and he will have wrongly awakened his audience's interest.

It will not help him, either, to try to characterize these as comic figures, giving them funny things to say. The would-be funny servant is almost always a deplorable character. Their humor—whether they be cockney, Irish or colored—is almost always based on the malapropism or the mispronunciation, and these things have ceased to be funny in the theater, except to the cheapest of audiences. I was given to using them for the servants of whom I wrote in my earlier plays. I have heard surprising examples of them in real life. A cook I had not long ago informed me that she was "bronical," and then added that "bronical was chronical." I could see myself, when I was younger, rushing for a pencil to make a note of that, inventing a cook in my next play who would use it. I know better now. I have learned to dread the cockney or the colored or the Irish voice when a stage maid opens her mouth. I dread things like "bronical is chronical" coming out. Freshness, impertinence or a kind of unctuous worldly wisdom are as bad. Do not do it. Leave it all alone.

You go to a friend's house, and the maid brings in the drinks. She may say, "Yes, sir," or relay a message that has been received, but she seldom emerges as a personality. You know nothing of her, and you need to know nothing of her. Let that normally be true on the stage as well; let the servant bring in the drinks, and then go. If she is a part of the plot, if her relationship with the other characters is important and a segment of the play, that is another thing. Then you must conceive her as a person, build her in your own head, spend as much time on inventing her as on anyone else. The main thing is to know from the start which characters are people, and which are dummies, in the way that the doorman and the hat-check girl may be dummies to you in real life, and to establish and stick to that distinction. The doorman is not a dummy to his wife, nor the hat-check girl to her boy-friend, but it is the author's job to know whether the play is about them in their professional or their personal situations. What is fatal is to start them as though they were people, make them part of your exposition and plot so that the audience becomes interested in them, and then to neglect them, leaving them as dead as if they were the chiffonier. If they are to be dummies, let them be dummies as they would be in real life, right from the beginning. In that way, neither interest nor time is lost. Both of these are essentials. You may not waste them.

CHAPTER EIGHT

Characters—I

I HAVE BEEN speaking of the lesser characters in plays, the ones that are dummies and should be, and the ones that should not. But the principal characters can be dummies, too. It has nothing to do with how much they have to do in the play. They can stay on stage for the whole evening, and still remain as dummy characters. By "dummies" here, I mean something perhaps a little different. I mean the people to whom things happen, people who actually do things that are important to the play, but who seem only to be manipulated into doing them by the author, who speak only his words, the obvious machine-made words—who, briefly, are never alive. Why does this happen?

The first answer is that the author has never conceived of them as real people, he has thought of them only in terms that reduce them to puppets answering his string-pulling. Probably, he has thought of his plot, first and foremost. That is one of the dangers of doing so. It is what is apt to happen in mystery stories, where the whole plot, the whole ingenuity of the poisoned chocolate murder, has been worked out without people first, and the need for characters is faced later. Then it will be found that almost any characters will fit. The hero, the heroine, the detective, the unrecognizable villain—maybe it would be a good idea to make him the local minister—some comic relief in the way of elderly aunts and prissy spinsters—these are what is needed, these are what will follow. A few touches of personal idiosyncrasy, a few extraneous bits of business—making the detective fond of cheap candy—may be added like a spicy sauce to some bad fish—but the fish will remain bad and tasteless all the same.

But this is not the only answer. There is another, which I think is insufficiently recognized. There is the danger of what is called "the straight character," which means, roughly, Mr. or Mrs. Blank, who signifies the average, typical, ordinary man and woman, the Mr. and Mrs. Blank anywhere. Here again, I want to come out with a firm and determined statement, this time in the words of the English playwright, Dodie Smith, who once told me categorically that "there was no such thing as a straight character, or at any rate that there should not be." I immediately accused her of having filled her plays with them, and added several of my own in addition. Her reply was that they were not straight parts, and that if they were, they should not have been. I know very well what she meant by this, and I heartily endorse it. There is no average Mr. or Mrs. Blank, at all. An attempt to draw one—for example, the ordinary middle-class husband or wife—will lead you into the pit of emptiness, and you will emerge with something as unreal as the juveniles in plays who come in impertinently swinging tennis rackets, and when the time for their exit arrives, make it with the remark: "Tennis, anyone?"

But, you will say, you are anxious to make your man or woman typical of every man or woman of that walk of life. Their story must be typical of every man or woman's story, and their reactions to it equally typical. They are to be Mr. Smith down the street from you, who catches the eight-forty morning train, or his wife, Mrs. Smith, who drives her children to school, goes home and listens to the soap operas (which are full of Mrs. Smiths just like her), plays bridge, cooks her husband's dinner, sits up and watches television with him in the evening, and goes to bed at ten-thirty, prepared for another day—a succession of other days—exactly the same. Yes, I know. It all looks as if it can be reduced to that, but it cannot. Those things are the externals. But, you will continue to object, if I give Mrs. Smith some personal distinction, some oddities, then she will no longer be *any* Mrs. Smith, she will become my personal Mrs. Smith, and the story which is to be the story of every Mrs. Smith in the world, will no longer be that. I must make my service man, in a wartime story, typical of *all* service men. I can only answer that if you try to do that, you will produce a character that is not an entity at all, that looks like all the typical service men on posters (who have never yet looked like any service man I have ever seen, if only for the fact that their teeth and features are too regular), and that sounds like the service men who speak on War Bond drives, who have seldom sounded like human beings either, saying only the regular and traditional things. You will have emptied that character of anything that makes him into a person. The same thing applies to the illustrations to slick-magazine stories, where the characters' appearance has been ironed out of everything individual into standard good looks.

I would like to take an illustration from *The Voice of the Turtle*. In Sally, the heroine of that play, I drew what I considered a somewhat odd girl. Or, rather, she drew herself for me. I liked her, I was amused by her, but there were times while she was writing herself, when she seemed to be getting close to being a goon-girl, a near half-wit, though she remained consistent and appealing. The one thing I never thought of her as being was Everywoman. I never thought she could be identified as Miss Smith. But she was. I have had letters and comments from women telling me that Sally was themselves, and asking how I could possibly have known so much about their insides and thoughts and dreams. The play had achieved that kind of universal identification that is every playwright's best desire, which can almost never be achieved by aiming at it. The man in the play seemed more usual to me, more like the ordinary man. Perhaps that is why he was less individual, and why few men have identified themselves with Bill Page. He managed, just, to escape from being characterless by a certain quality of wit, of observation and detachment, a slightly rueful bitterness, loneliness and sensitivity, but he was a less interesting character than Sally was.

Now this proved something to me that I had long suspected. Do not worry over your character's apparent oddities, if they seem real and truthful to you, and most certainly do not worry over their interfering with the character's identification with the members of the audience. They will help it. You want the hero to be the typical businessman. Do you know the typical businessman? You know what he looks like, what he wears, but these things are not the man. Do not stick to the essentials. Do your best to avoid them, give him thoughts that you think the typical business man might not have, interests that he might not have, daydreams that he might not have. Make him further and further from the apparently typical man in the insurance advertisements, and he will emerge exactly as you want him, and all the businessmen you meet will come and tell you how extraordinarily well you have drawn them. Never call him Mr. Smith. You might just as well call him Mr. X or Mr. Y or Mr. Z. Call him an unlikely name, a name that the average businessman would seem unlikely to own, and let the name help you to a character, if you cannot get it any other way. Sir Arthur Pinero always had odd names for his characters: Tanqueray, Ebbsmith, Panmure, Jesson, Queckett. He named a manicurist—presumably the straight character, the "any manicurist" character—Sophie Fullgarney. Within the limits of the play, she is a real and true character, and she is individually conceived as a person. I am sure that a great many manicurists—or girls who were earning their livings—saw her as being exactly true of themselves.

One gets into the way of thinking of the lesser roles as being characters, and of the leading parts as being straight. This is a mistake, springing perhaps from a decayed memory of stock-company casting, or of the leading man or woman who depended on their personal charms as well as on their tailors or dressmakers for their appeal. The few, the very few, leading men and women today who can add something to a blank part, some personal magnetism, an audience appeal of their own, can fool you into thinking that you have managed something as author, but you have not. You have still created only the vacuum, known as a straight part. If you draw fascinating and witty women and do not give them witty lines to speak, you are counting on the leading lady, with her charm and her reputation, to do the job for you. There are few actresses who can. These vacuum parts, too, are more likely to happen when one is drawing either an exceptionally brilliant person, or a "good" character. The author's imagination fails to depict or perhaps to conceive brilliance, and it fails to depict and to conceive real goodness, too. The man or woman who is resistant to or oblivious of temptation is as hard to draw as a saint. They will almost always emerge as prigs. The state of mind that produces goodness is a hard one to envision, and the writer's imagination produces only a flat, level country of disinterestedness in anything human. Bad people are easier to draw, perhaps because the authors share, to some extent, their temperaments. Their badness gives them whatever the opposite of straightness is—their curvature, perhaps. One can envision badness, invent its details. Goodness should be as positive and as flaming, though it seldom emerges in literature in that way. The real trouble lies in having conceived the character as good, in having labeled him and his quality in your mind, instead of creating an individual.

If you have failed in every other way to see Mrs. Smith as more than the typical suburban housewife, then I would suggest that you try to see her for a moment in terms of an actress, a specific actress, or better in terms of a number of specific actresses, all of whom are of the age to play her, and then realize how different she would be in each case. She will still be Mrs. Smith, but she will no longer be the Mrs. Smith of the cake-baking advertisements. I do not mean that you should write her as a part for one of these actresses; I have mentioned them merely to show you that Mrs. Smith can be perfectly individual; they may help an individual woman to start coming into your head. Hang on to that individual woman, create her and then write her.

Take some of the best characters you have met in plays, and have a look at them. Take the people out of J. M. Barrie, all of whom are keyed with a very sharp touch of strangeness; take the women out of *Our Betters* by Somerset Maugham; take more modern ones, like Laura and Amanda in *The Glass Menagerie* and Blanche Dubois in *A Streetcar Named Desire*. Take the men in the latter play, Stanley Kowalski and Mitch; take Willy Loman in *Death of a Salesman;* take Berenice and Frankie in *The Member of the Wedding*. To go backward again, take the three leads in Emlyn Williams' *Night Must Fall* and the leads in *The Corn Is Green;* all the men in *Journey's End;* the leads in *Idiot's Delight;* the men in *The Green Bay Tree;* the vivid figures in Sidney Howard's *They Knew What They Wanted;* the horror-charged people in *The Little Foxes;* almost anyone at all out of James Bridie—what do you realize? These are all character parts, vividly unlike the so-called ordinary man and woman, yet so alive that you cannot forget them, and so universal that you are always meeting people like them.

Star parts are different, was the old answer. The star wanted all the sympathy, all the romance that the author could supply. That is no longer true. Almost all the parts I have listed above are star parts nowadays. Stars have become actors, too. That is a fine thing, which means that they can fit into plays, instead of having plays woven around them, as webs for them to sit in.

I like that. I think the play must come first. And to make the play, the people must be living, and to be living they must be character parts. Everyone one meets in life is a character part. Never forget that.

There are other things I want to say about character-drawing. I want to warn any author never to fall in love with a character. That is another reason why good characters are so hard to draw, they have been conceived too lovingly, and therefore too respectfully. This is responsible, too, for some of the more irritating female figures in dramatic literature—the author's decision that he was writing a fine, noble and wholly admirable woman. It explains a good deal of self-pity in heroines, because the pity was the author's. It explains some of those overfine and oversensitive women, of whom Laura in *Young Woodley* was one. It is—or was, when she was a more frequent figure than she now is—the reason for those suffering women who always seem to have been looking the other way when they allowed themselves to get married, and spend most of their stage life backing against the bedroom door when their husbands want their conjugal rights—women who, in the words of G. B. Stern, behave like shot pheasants. The author has fallen in love with a not very real form of sacrificed femininity. These are the women who, in the description of Somerset Maugham, never have to go to the bathroom. It would shock their authors to think that they did. Consider your heroine going to the bathroom, would be a good maxim.

When lady authors fall in love with their male characters, an excess of masculine virility is discharged, of the kind that led Max Beerbohm to suspect in public that Rudyard Kipling was really a woman in disguise. The men written by women, Beerbohm remarked, "tremble at the sound of their own footsteps, fearing that the soles of their boots are not heavy enough. In ever-present dread of a sudden soprano note in the bass, they tremble at the sound of their own voices. Their language must be strong, but sparse. No babbling fountains must they be, but volcanoes of whose inner fires we are to catch through infrequent cracks terrific glimpses. In real life, men are not like that. At least, only the effeminate men are like that. The others have no preoccupation with manliness." If you fall in love with your characters, you will let them become patronizing, so that they say things like: "You wouldn't understand," when asked why they have behaved as maddeningly as they have. They will have no desires at all, merely principles. They will sacrifice anything for their principles. I think even that sanest of writers, Granville Barker, fell in love with the overprincipled heroine of *The Voysey Inheritance.*

Authors can fall in love with disreputable women, too, in which case they usually manage to glorify their disreputableness. The noble tart who takes care of a sick sister, the prostitute who reads Plato and Plotinus in her spare time, are usually the result of an author's infatuation. Children were, too, in the older type of play. The author had fallen in love with their innocence and cuteness, wanting the audience to share that emotion, and killing them quite relentlessly to produce the requisite tears. Dickens had shown the way to that. Mother figures are another example of this, when the author has not decided to hate them. I drew Mama in *I Remember Mama* from Miss Kathryn Forbes's book, and I was spared infatuation with her because

Miss Forbes had avoided it, but on the first day of rehearsals I warned Miss Mady Christians that neither of us was to fall in love with the figure from then on.

Hate can do the same kind of harm. It is bad for an author to hate his characters; it distorts his vision. I have always thought that Sidney Howard came very close to spoiling *The Silver Cord* because he almost hated Mrs. Phelps and would not give her a fair showing. I think that I hated the schoolmaster in *Young Woodley* as much as I was in love with his wife, though I did my best to make amends in *The Druid Circle* where I drew a similar character with more complexity and more compassion, I hope. What the author needs is detachment, a kind of Godlike quality toward his people. He need not see them all as glowing with goodness, but he must neither love nor hate them humanly. He must know more than that about them. One of the best examples of this is *Hedda Gabler*. Hedda is a dislikable woman, but Ibsen never expended an ounce of hatred toward her. He knew her, he pitied her, he made her explainable and therefore tragic. This is the ideal to be aimed at.

Lastly, I think the characters must all be kept in the same key, as the play must. It is dangerous to conceive half of one's characters as real, and half of them in a cynical or satiric vein. The author should set the mood of a play, and stick to his own vision in it. If he is drawing a picture of vice and a vicious world, he must be sure what is his attitude and what is the attitude that he wants the audience to take toward it. It is very dangerous to shift ground. This happens mainly because the author is unsure of whether the audience will appreciate his own right feelings. He draws vicious characters, but for some reason they become attractive. He wants the audience to know for certain that, despite that fact, his own heart is in the right place. He therefore introduces a good character who can say all the right, the true, the proper things. This does not always work out. The hard-boiledness, if properly handled, has taken its own hold, and the audience is charmed by it, has caught its mood. It will not willingly listen to the author's sermons delivered by anyone.

Despite my warning that I was not going to take examples of what I thought bad in the plays of anyone else, I would like to depart from that ruling now to illustrate this last point. I think that Somerset Maugham will not too strongly object to this, since it comes in a play of his I otherwise admire enormously—*Our Betters*. In that play he is engaged in portraying the immoral and dissolute lives of American girls who have married into European society, and he does so through two very brilliant women's characters. The play is a battle between Pearl Grayson and Minnie, Duchesse de Surennes. The interest of the plot turns on the audience watching them fighting with each other, deeply fascinated by their struggles, and hoping—there is no way out of it, once you have embroiled the audience—that the worse of the two will win. The worse one does win. That is fine. Pearl's triumph over her rival and also over her own protector at the last curtain of the play is exactly what is needed.

But where I think that Maugham made his mistake was to include some virtuous characters as well. There are really three or four of them, but only two seriously count. There is a sad and wise commentator in the Princess who knows the mistake she has made, and is gentle and generous about the others, and there is the charming virgin sister of Pearl. When the play starts, Bessie is admiring of her sister; when it ends, she knows Pearl for what she is, and returns to America without her. Bessie is the touchstone, the good girl, the mouthpiece of goodness for the audience. She is there to show them the right side. But she does damage. If one has come to watch the battle of the two women with interest, and to want to see Pearl win it, then Bessie becomes a bore. If one takes Bessie sympathetically, then the battle becomes offensive, and the play repulsive. In the theater, Bessie was a slight bore.

I have seen this quite often in plays. It happens very seldom in French ones, where the audience is naturally more cynical and more inclined to satire. English and American writers are more wary, more fearful of their own reputations, they want to be quite sure that the audience knows that they know right from wrong. That is how those other characters creep in, and help to mix the moods. A similar mixing can happen without the aid of new characters; the existing ones can seem suddenly to change sides, as the author's heart seems to change. A vein of sentimentality creeps in the moment that the watchdog of toughness or cynicism goes to sleep. This I have found to be a rather American characteristic, a sudden swoop to the noble and the sacrificial, to a whole scale of traditional theater values when the lid is removed. The top crust of the pie is lifted, and there is a mushiness below, which is the author's own mushiness, true or assumed for virtue, and the play descends rapidly. There is lemon meringue filling, after all. One has started with satire, and ended with Pollyanna.

sixteen who adored him. At the end of a longish scene, i
ich he played no part, the boy went off, suddenly, into a fain
ad meant this faint merely as a sign of relaxed tension, a
stration of the strain the boy had been under, waiting for th
dict, and for the brief scene between himself and the hero
ding and affectionate, on his recovery. It was a detail t
ate atmosphere and personal relationship only. I was amazed
he number of people who took it as an indication—a very
ar indication—that I meant the boy to have committed the
rder, a sign for me to the audience that he was the guilty
ty. I am still bitter about that. (But then I am a little bitter
ut that play. Its basic device seems to have been something
t an audience will not swallow, and I knew that we were sunk
en, after the opening while the actors were taking their bows,
oman in the gallery called out: "Who did it?" I had thought
t I had made it quite plain that the play was not a detective
ry, and that the identity of the murderer was in no way
ntial to its theme. The audience would not accept that fact.)
fainting was intended as a detail only, but it was, appar-
ly, the wrong detail to have chosen. Remember, too, that one
wo details in a play will do what several chapters can do in
vel, and be sure you pick the right ones.
This leads to another question—how much of the past lives
our characters should you tell about, how much, even,
uld you know, quite apart from what you present? What
ut those notebooks, of which we sometimes hear, filled with
r past histories? Too much past detail in an author's mind
be a bad thing. My suggestion here—if it seems to mean
thing—is that the author should know, or be able to answer
stions about, everything concerning his characters, but that

CHAPTER NINE

Characters—II

FROM NOW ON, one of your main concerns is going to be selectiveness. You are going to have to choose every detail with care; you are going to have to be selective in your choice of characters. You may have five aunts of your own, all of whom you would like to put into that family play, especially if you have conceived it as "the family play to end all family plays." You will find that all five cannot go in. They will cancel each other out, the audience will not be able to see one because of the others. The theatrical vision is limited. The five will be reduced to two, or at most to three; the others will have to wait for another play, or their characteristics must be blended with those belonging to the ones you keep. I started a play once with a scene between two old ladies who were teachers of singing. I was enchanted with what I wrote for them. It was only when I had finished it that I knew it took me nowhere that I wanted to go. Singing and a taste for music were adjuncts and decorations, in no way a part of my story. Two old ladies discussing them were too many. Out went the second one, never to be used again, although many of the things she had to say were embodied in the one who remained.

This process of elimination will go on throughout your play. One of the first things to learn in playwriting is just how much an audience needs to send its imagination where you want it to go. Take, for instance, the matter of lovers, how many your heroine should have had. This will vary to some extent from time to time. There was a quite well-known play produced in London in the nineteen-twenties, in which a mature woman, unmarried, confessed to having had lovers. In the original script she admitted to three. When the play was performed, I think the number was reduced to one. There is a lot to be learned from this. At that time, in the theater (always, as Bernard Shaw pointed out in the eighteen-nineties, a good twenty years behind current morality) it was unusual, slightly shocking, for an unmarried woman to confess to lovers. One, therefore, was sufficient to establish her as a free-thinking and free-living woman. Two would have made her generous. Three would have made her a tart.

I am not being funny here. I mean it sincerely. You will have to gauge your audience, and the time that your play is presented. Remember those lovers, and then remember your own mother, your unmarried great-aunt, the girl you last had an affair with, the easygoing rip, and the Minister from back home. They will all form part of your audience. You have got to appeal to them all, suggest the same thing to them all, in so far as that is possible. Then count your lovers again. Never mind how many you are sure the lady had. Use only enough to let your mixed audience get the same idea.

There are two other illustrations of the heroine can have. One is from *The Secon There, rather to my astonishment when I Paula is described before her entrance as gentleman protectors. (There was also Hu the plot and is kept very quiet about until the very great many for 1893. But Paula was moved from man to man. In a play of my *ance,* one of the two leading ladies was a w married, who had had a fairly well-known l ond act, the young girl asks her about her l know if there have been a lot. The reply is: thing that no two people would agree about lot." The laugh that greeted that reply ind had hit exactly where I wanted to, and al just the right impression of her life without numbers at all. It would be interesting to b audiences, and see how the estimate of nun minds.

The same thing is true of all the deta characters' lives. However real these detail be quite sure of their necessity and their val will prove before you use them. Remember ways listens. It listens far better and far believe, and it expects every single detail to suggest something. Nothing can be ther the audience will be waiting to see just wh this out bitterly in *Somebody Knows.* The was about an unsolved murder. The hero had a scene in the witnesses' waiting room free man. Among the family that was waiti

he should not consciously have thought it out. If you will develop in your head that early, frustrated engagement to the Vicar's son when your heroine was only seventeen, you will find it hard not to use it, not to refer to it when you are writing, and it may very well have nothing to do with what you are telling. The same difficulty occurs in dramatizing too long novels, with all the chapters and incidents you find hard to forget. It occurred to me, too, in *The Damask Cheek,* where I had invented an almost incredible amount of detail concerning my heroine; I had given her two sisters, both married, with details of whom they married, a past engagement of her own, and two married cousins in America. These all came into the first script, and all had to be scraped off again like barnacles. The small bits that remained were valuable, carefully selected for that purpose. The Christmas party at which, aged nine, she had lost her temper and bashed another girl over the head, this episode stayed in the play. It was a plant for her temper-losing scene in the last act, a symbol of her regret that she was not as good-looking as other girls, and of her early developed love for the hero, which was why she attacked the girl in the prettier fancy dress. But you cannot have many of those incidents.

Also, do not if you can avoid it (and you can) have a wholly irrelevant tale told on the stage, even if it is to point a moral for your play. This was one of Sir Arthur Pinero's favorite tricks. He was fond of *raisonneur* characters, characters who are there merely to be told the facts and then to comment on them, work them into a significant shape and reason the whole thing out for the audience. Never have *raisonneurs* in modern plays, and particularly not in propaganda plays; they are always given not so much to making speeches as to speechifying. In *His House in*

Order, Pinero makes his *raisonneur* relate a very long story about a French chef who blew himself and his kitchen up because he was always being compared to his predecessor. The point of the story is a parallel between the two wives of Filmer Jesson, which is the center of the play, but the moment that Hilary starts on his anecdote, the spirits of the audience fall (or they do today), and one can visualize the spirits of the other actors falling, too. "Bear with me awhile while I tell you a story," is something no one should be submitted to in a theater any longer.

In handling characters and their pasts, another point raises itself in my mind. This is the question of time and timeliness. For the most part, plays are written of today. "Time—the present" is on most programs, or supposed to be. When it is not, there is often a deeper reason than one suspects. The present time may well be all awry for the author. The years we are living in are ill-timed for the gentler and more reflective writer, who needs a sense of security and continuance in the world around him, and not the fear and uncertainty of our present existence. He longs for the years before 1914 when it seemed as though the quality of life could never change, or the years between the wars when he could still hope that it would not. Today he, and all his characters, are beset with anxiety. That is why there are more plays set in a past period than there used to be, or why authors struggle so hard to avoid naming the date or nailing it down.

Once you determine to set your play today, you are bound by certain details which seem at their best irrelevant, and at their worst insuperable. This was a severe problem during the war. A play written in 1943 was obstructed by all sorts of problems, quite apart from why the hero was not in uniform. There was the gas problem alone. People could not move from one place to another by car without the audience wondering where they got the gas. In England the food problem must have operated (and must still operate) equally strongly. To some extent, these problems can remain forever. After World War I, it was impossible to write a play in England without being able to account for what the men were doing between 1914 and 1918. The same will be true of men anywhere today. As the war recedes in time, the problems will lessen, but there will always be remnants. The young man of seventeen today will have to face being called up for military service very soon. You cannot, as a playwright, ignore that fact and plan his future as you would once have done.

How much is the author bound by these things, to what extent must he follow them? If he does follow them, he is apt to date his play. The gas problem will vanish, and if it is essential to the plot, then his play will seem localized and lessened in importance. The play may become outmoded as *Ned McCobb's Daughter* was outmoded by the abolition of prohibition. If the author does not follow them, then his play may be unproducible while the conditions last. The best he can do is to dodge them when he can, skirt them, avoid them, try to see his play unlocalized in time, turning his eyes away from detail. It is easier to do than you would expect; it involves a general widening of vision, a less topical viewpoint. There will be exceptions, and those will be unfortunate.

There is another question related to this one, and there I have no hesitation in giving an answer. This is the permissibility of using real names, names of people and places, to create atmosphere or to get laughs. I would say that it is impermissible. That form of humor or identification belongs to revue, and not to the legitimate theater. But, says the young writer, I need to mention the leading musical conductor, or the leading actress of the moment, in order to make a point concerning my struggling hero or heroine. It will save me so much time if I can mention Toscanini or Katharine Cornell, instead of having to invent someone whom the audience will never recognize as clearly in their place. I still say, "Don't"—evade the issue, do it some other way. Do not let your actress heroine have spent hours waiting in the Shubert office, or have been presented with a letter of introduction to Rodgers and Hammerstein. There are several reasons for my firmness about this, and they are not all because the Shuberts and even Rodgers and Hammerstein will pass, and your play, we hope, can remain. There is a slight distastefulness, a slight rubbing-the-wrong-way of the audience's feelings when it is done, even if a laugh results. The two media have become mixed—real life and stage life. It is no good saying that they are always mixed, and that there is no objection to your referring to the White House, and even perhaps to its then incumbent. I cannot answer that in satisfactory detail, but I do know that mention of real people—and in a lesser degree of real places, which are anything less than permanent—does the one thing that one is aiming not to do: it reminds the audience that it is in a theater. The author is winking just a little, nudging it and saying: "You know." Invent a producer, a stage star, if you must (I have done it myself, and I have never been very pleased with it), but do not use the real one. If you are deliberately setting your play backward in date, and are making use of the names you have chosen as a part of your special background, then it can be permissible—though, remember here Max Beerbohm's "Savonarola" Brown, who wrote a play of Florence in the fifteenth century, packed all the celebrated figures into walk-ons, and added "Pippa Passes" as a stage direction. A reference to Ellen Terry or to Sarah Bernhardt will be all right for a play set in the nineties, but a mention of Mary Martin in a play set today will not. That may well be why you have decided to antedate your play. It may postdate less easily that way. It is not a bad reason. The past at least is secure.

Lastly, we come to the off-stage characters. These have long been a preoccupation of mine, and I have loved them for many years, other people's as well as my own. I think now that it was a rather childish preoccupation. I liked to use them, to scatter them all over my plays. There was an off-stage family called the Barringers, who always had the house and the parties to which my characters went. I could, and still can, list you the names of a hundred or more off-stage people in well-known plays. I had an argument with a critic who swore that I was wrong in naming Candida's children among them. Candida, the critic swore, had no children. There would have been no play if she had had. I pointed to three lines in Act One referring to the fact that they were away in the country, getting over scarlatina, and that it was from them that Candida returned at the opening. The critic answered that there were still no children. Shaw had mentioned them as a device merely, and had then forgotten them again, as Shakespeare forgot the babe to which Lady Macbeth had given suck, once he had mentioned it. To this I agreed. Candida has, to all intents and purposes, no children.

But off-stage characters can have value, a great deal of value, if selectively handled. Again, I say, as few as possible. Pick them with care, imagine them well, and they can do more for you than they could had they been brought on. I am proud of Mrs. de Pass, the off-stage head-witch, in *Bell, Book and Candle*. She is a part of the plot, she is well described, she is funny enough to get laughs when mentioned, we know what her apartment looks like, and she is far better left off, devised by the audience from hints, than she would have been had I brought her on. The characters of the theatrical producer and the Naval Commander helped to people the stage and to thicken the three-personed cast of *The Voice of the Turtle*. One of my favorite of all off-stage characters was invented by George Kelly in *The Fatal Weakness*. This is Minerva Nichols, the friend of Mrs. Wentz, who does all the off-stage spying and trailing of the defaulting husband. Minerva has her own car, and absolutely *nothing* else to do. She is a magnificent invention, and counts with the best visible characters in modern drama.

Shakespeare used off-stage characters more than is suspected, quite apart from Lady Macbeth's obscure child. Mr. Curdle, whom we have mentioned before, had written a pamphlet of sixty-four pages on the character of the Nurse's deceased husband in *Romeo and Juliet*, inquiring whether he really was a merry man in his lifetime, or whether it was only his widow's affectionate partiality that induced her so to describe him. This, considering there is only one mention of him in the play, is typical of the Mr. Curdles of this world, and is also a symptom of what I meant when I said that my own preoccupation with off-stage characters was a childish one. I think Mr. Curdle a little childish. The Nurse refers to her husband because she is a rattle, and needs to chatter about Juliet's childhood and the joke he made when Juliet fell on her face. It is a little infantile to start delving into his qualities as a person.

There is another off-stage character in Shakespeare, who seems to me to illustrate a further use to which such people can be put. She comes into *Othello,* and she is Desdemona's mother's maid, called Barbara. She taught Desdemona the "Willow Song," which is almost certainly why Shakespeare created her, if you want to be technical about it. (And the "Willow Song" may very well only be there because the boy playing Desdemona sang very charmingly, and was temperamental and would not play the part if there were not a song for him.) But having invented her, Shakespeare makes use of her in a fascinating way. You could lose her and lose nothing of the essential quality of *Othello,* but she serves most poignantly to bring the tragedy down to human dimensions when it seems to be soaring almost too high. This is one of the things (like his sense of humor even in his tragedies) which makes Shakespeare so great. We see Desdemona suddenly in relation to her own past, as we can look back from the eminence of any given moment of our own lives and marvel at the continuity that has wound the thread of our fate from the days of childhood until now. "Poor Barbara," as Desdemona calls her, who must have known and played with her as a baby, is a symbol and a humanizing factor in a situation that might well have seemed too inhuman and removed from life without her.

But valuable as they are, a playwright can go too far with these off-stage characters as he can with on-stage ones. He can pile them on in an attempt to create an atmosphere of reality, and after a very few of them have been mentioned, the audience stops paying any attention. It can no longer visualize or believe in them. It is hard to make an audience pay attention to details about any people it has not seen; it can be done, with great selectiveness, about one, seldom more than one. Even if your characters are to appear later, reserve your details and your comments about them, if possible, until after they have done so; they will be better remembered.

There is also the off-stage character who is one of the main persons in the play, the character whom the play is all about, but who never appears. This was the main gimmick of *Edward, My Son,* where the audience never saw Edward at all. It has been used several times, occasionally for dead characters whose names provide the play with its title—*Rebecca,* for instance, dramatized from the novel. In England (until *Victoria Regina*) it was a necessity for the Royal Family, their relatives and their more or less recent forebears. It is true, almost anywhere, of Jesus Christ. The continued devices in *Family Portrait* to keep Him off stage suggested to me that the play would have been better entitled *He Just Stepped Out for a Moment.* The device is a not invaluable one, but the fact that it so apparently is one is something to its discredit. The audience is aware that the author is pulling something, indulging in a trick, and the play, no matter how successful, is slightly cheapened. It becomes a method of sleight of hand, rather than a play.

I would say, too, that it is unwise to complicate your characters with family relationships more involved than is usual. Half-brothers, children by the same parents of separate marriages from each, these are hard things for an audience to follow. In the same way and for the same reason, try to avoid calling your people by names that are too hard to separate from each other. Robert and Richard have a similarity to me, though Bob and

Dick have not. Try to name them so that they can be remembered. Names for characters are of great importance to me. I spend at least a day, and often more, on them. I search my memory, the telephone directory, the register of my old schoolfellows, trying to find the right ones. I cannot start writing a character until I have the right name for it. I started *Leave Her to Heaven* with the heroine named Daisy. After three pages, I realized that she would not come to life for me. I thought again, tried over other names in my head, looking for one that was both middle-class and suburban, and which also had a slightly flashy and glittering sound for me. I ended with Madge, and after that she gave me no trouble.

This may well be personal to me, though I think it is the contrary that is unusual. A playwright of my acquaintance once read to me the draft of a first act in which the characters were listed as Y. S., E. S., E. S. 's Wife, Mother and Father. The initials stood for Younger Son and Elder Son. To me, such a proceeding would have been impossible, and I think that most authors feel as I do. G. B. Stern, when she wrote her novel, *The Matriarch*, named, in the family tree at the end of the book, her heroine's husband (a character who never appeared) as Maurice. Later, she wrote a sequel dealing with the marriage, and here the husband was called Giles, with an explanation that Maurice was his real first name, but that he was never called by it. When I asked her about this, she explained that the man she wanted to write could never—to her—have been named Maurice. It would have been possible, she admitted, to have written him as Giles and then to have had a secretary substitute Maurice *passim*, but she would never have been able to look at or think about the book without distaste. I understand and share her feelings completely. I know why Pinero used the names that he did, and I have used some odder ones, myself. They have and give to the characters a real individuality. I think they also help the audience to remember them more vividly.

And lastly, there are certain questions of practicality that cannot be omitted. The author must consider how well he can get his parts played. Once it would have been wise to suggest that he omit children if he could do so. Stage children were impossible. Legal rulings make them impossible after certain hours in England still. Today, however, in America (apart from Washington where the legal rulings are even stricter) this theory has broken down. John Henry in *The Member of the Wedding* is superbly castable now, and an astonishing number of good child actors can suddenly be found. But there are other points to be remembered. Do not write a part that demands an actor or actress of star quality, and then use it for only one scene. You will never find an actor who can play it, whose salary you can afford. I have done this once, and I know. Remember that beauty and personal magnetism in anyone over thirty are apt to make the possessor a star either on Broadway or in Hollywood, and do not, therefore, write a part that demands both or either of the two qualities to project it, and have it be anything less than a star role. The actor will not be there, and the person who will ultimately play it will be deficient in just the qualities you most need. Remember that actors are jealous people, and that if the leading woman's part in a play is (or seems) too good and too showy, you will have a great deal of trouble finding a man romantic and attractive enough to play opposite to her. He will tell you—they will all tell you—that the play belongs to the woman. This has happened to me three times at least, and the resulting search for someone who will play it is a long and discouraging one, as you slide further and further downhill, from name to lesser name, and to the man you once saw in summer stock. You can always get character actors, you can usually get young men and women, but the field for lesser than star parts for maturer people is a bad one. You will only find the failures, and you will soon learn why they were failures.

I do not mean by this that you should try to cast your parts when you write them. I consider that a bad idea; it both limits you and will ultimately disappoint you; but it is a good idea to know, roughly, what you will be able to get. Once again, your play depends on being performed, and as well performed as can be managed. There is no point in increasing your troubles in advance. There will be enough of them, anyway.

CHAPTER TEN

Dialogue—I

BUT YOUR characters must talk. Speech is the essence of the drama. This is not so in talking pictures where the author is still begged to keep his dialogue to a minimum. If information cannot be got across in any other way, it is finally put over in the form of dialogue, but this is always felt to be a slight failure on somebody's part. I am not complaining of this. I think the movies are right in this decision. A long flow of talk is dull in pictures, and they have good reason to remember their silent background. But the decision makes for certain keen differences between the two arts, and one of them is in the delineation of character. Speaking very broadly, there are no characters in movies. There is no time to build them. The names of movie characters (unless derived from plays or novels) will not remain with you as do, for example, those of the heroes and heroines of good plays. You will remember only the actor or actress who played them. The smaller points of personal intimacy that only dialogue can establish have no place in screen fare. To the movie writer, dialogue is really of two kinds only. Either it must make a point—a plot point—or it must make a crack, a funny crack or a sentimental crack or a message crack. If it tries merely to color or create a personage, there will be no room for it. Let the theater and the playwright remember this; it is to their benefit that it is so.

But speech is almost the only thing that the theater can use, the more so since spectacles and highly scenic dramas have lost their popularity, because the movies can do them so much better. The quality of speech, the kind of dialogue to be employed is, therefore, of the greatest importance to the writer. It behooves me, therefore, to write about it, and it is the most difficult of all subjects to handle or to describe. What is good dialogue? What are its essentials?

There are many different kinds of dialogue. Every author has his own kind, and actually must have it. It is very odd, but without losing at all the power to create characters, to make them talk recognizably and differently, almost every first-class playwright has his own special sound in his writing. His own voice echoes in it, and I think that I could—from not more than two pages—give a pretty shrewd guess at the author of any script, if he were a well-known writer. As I write that phrase, it reminds me of someone. Of whom? Of Somerset Maugham. "A pretty shrewd guess." That is a Maugham phrase. So is "I have a notion." Yet Maugham writes very good dialogue, but he writes it as only he himself could. This is an interesting point. Dialogue, then, is not merely representative of the character, it is representative of the author, too, as every actor's performance is not only a portrait of the character he is playing, but is tinged, at least, with his own voice, his own facial expressions, his own personality. Many of us would wish that this were not true. I, myself, know the sound of my own voice in my dialogue, and I frequently wish it were not there, as I wish that my own face did not stare back at me from the shaving mirror each morning. But if I try to avoid it, it means usually that I am writing only a pastiche of someone else, or else that it will have no distinguishable sound to it at all. The style of dialogue is like a novelist's style. It has its own sound, which is the sound of the author. One would have thought that this would not have been true of reported speech, but it apparently is. You will have to trust your own face and your own voice in the end.

One can, of course, mold those, change them a little. When very young, one is apt to have no style, no personal quality, merely a series of echoes. As one matures, the personal habit forms. Soon, it is set. When children write plays, there is dialogue of the briefest and most factual kind only. "Here comes the Princess. I love her, but I am not noble. She cannot marry me. Exit." Later, the child learns to expand a little. Presently, he learns to write dialogue. My own dialogue is considered one of my better qualities, but, when I was in my later teens, my mother, talking to me of my playwriting, told me that my dialogue was so poor. It was. How did it become better? What were its faults? Was it bad, then, all on its own, or because it was unlike the kind of dialogue that my mother was accustomed to hearing in the theater? The answer to that is that it was bad for both reasons.

Let me go back a little, to a slightly earlier drama. When I was writing *The Damask Cheek,* I wanted to be sure of the sound of dialogue of that place and period—New York City in

1909. I turned to novels and to plays written then to remind me of it. I found almost nothing. Dialogue was seldom written in vernacular, I discovered. The plays of Clyde Fitch have almost no trace of Americanism in their locution, save in their lowest-class characters, and might as well have been written by Sir Arthur Pinero. Reread Pinero, and you will wonder (as well you might) whether people ever talked like that. Those long-winded sentences, carefully balanced as to construction, declaiming that the circumstances, however dubious they might appear, did not necessarily bear the interpretation that was so uncharitably being forced upon them—did people, other than pompous old gentlemen, really speak like that? It was a tradition of the theater that they did, a tradition that such critics as Bernard Shaw, Max Beerbohm and A. B. Walkley were always trying to break. I think that my mother was used to it, and perhaps to her ears dialogue ought to have sounded like that. It is well to remember this tradition, and the fact that it is past now. The best examples of it come, perhaps, not from the theater, but from Charles Dickens, whose characters talk superbly well and realistically until emotion hits them, whereupon they descend to flights of nonrealistic prose. Look at the speeches of Rosa Dartle to Little Emily. Today the author's ear must be perfectly attuned to the idiom of his characters' speech, and he must not mix it with his own, even though his own voice will still sound through it. Every person that he writes has his own way of speaking, his own vocabulary, and the author must keep a permanent watch not to step outside that, not to use words and phrases for characters that they would not employ in life.

There were other traditions of dialogue formerly, as well. There was the tradition of the epigram—the smart and univer-

sal generalization about life or men or women—so popularized
by Oscar Wilde, who invented better ones than anybody. Comedies had to have epigrams. Authors might well have carried
notebooks in those days, and have jotted these down as they
occurred to them. They could be moved with the greatest of
ease from play to play. Speeches beginning "All men" or "Any
woman" or "The conventions of Society are" prepared the
audience to laugh. Moments of great emotion demanded the
set speeches—a sudden flow of well-worded, carefully balanced
phrases, metaphors and similes, pouring out in a great torrent.
There were the sermon speeches, too, usually from the *raisonneur*, to set things straight. And they were all well written, in
the sense that the author had taken care in the choice and ar-
rangement of his words, as though he were writing a slightly
purple passage of prose. I have looked at some of these older
plays, and have twice asked older actresses who had known
and worked in that period, to read me a showier passage from
Oscar Wilde or Pinero, to let me hear how they sounded. Sur-
prisingly, in each case, they succeeded. They brought in a technique which is of no use today, and delivered the speeches
broadly and ringingly. It was not acting of the kind we now can
use or even, for the most part, appreciate, but it was acting. It
stirred me to listen to it.

It may even be that one day it will come back, that playwrights will get tired of the clipped and realistic modern utter-
ances, and long for the full and free speeches of the older
playwrights. There has been a slight movement toward this in
the revival of verse drama. When it fully happens, all our players
will have to take lessons in how to speak their lines. Another
technique will be demanded, and when a technique is needed, it

will appear. That is one of the miracles of life. But at the moment, most of our players can speak Pinero no more easily than they can speak Shakespeare and Congreve. I am talking now of America.

But there is a theory, springing from this, that I would like to nail on its head, a theory about the literary play, which is sometimes half-apologetically described as a play with good writing, but not good theater, as though that were an excuse for it. I think that if such a thing exists, it has mistaken its medium, and that the theater is no place for good writing, just as such. I know that bad theater means a bad play, and that good writing cannot redeem it. I want never to hear such a description of anything that I may write. Theater must come first, and the phrase "good theater" should never be used purely derogatively. Good theater is good entertainment, which is what plays are aimed at being; it can be impoved by good style, but good style without it is of no value. This is as true of the play in verse as it is of the play in prose. The literary conceits are still literary conceits, and have no theatrical merits on their own.

That they can have a place beside the other virtues I am not denying. As adjuncts they can be deeply valuable. A certain number of plays have flung themselves too much to the opposite extreme, adhering to their theme and only their theme with a puritan narrowness. I reread Stanley Houghton's *Hindle Wakes* a day or two ago. This was a play famous in its time as one of the severe Manchester school of drama that came into being around 1912. It contained a heroine who must have been one of the first in drama to refuse to be made an honest woman of by the rich young man with whom she had spent a week end "just for fun." It was a good play, and it was a valiant play, and a stern play technically. There is no line of dialogue and no moment of situation in it which does not bear directly on the seduction and the plot that resolves very simply from it. It seems now a little too tight, too tense, too unrelieved. The dialogue is good, but it is sparse and devoid of any variety. A touch or two of exterior, almost irrelevant, detail or characterization would help it. It is all too much on the nose, and a few literary or dramatic conceits would do it no harm. It was a play of a period of dramatic revolution, and it went a little far, a little too far. It could be used as an example of that.

It uses dialogue in idiom, of course. The play is set among the working classes in Lancashire, and the characters speak as their real-life prototypes would. Anyone who wants to know the Lancashire idiom could use it as a textbook. Or perhaps they could not, any longer. I do not know how much that idiom has changed in the years. There is a certain value for this reason in the kind of dialogue that is written without vernacular. The plays are apt to last longer. Nothing can date a play as fast as slang can. The few moments where Bernard Shaw has permitted it to himself—the "aints" and "ever so's" of *Mrs. Warren's Profession*—are the moments when we find it hard to see his people as real ones. When they talk Shavian dialogue (as special a kind as has ever been invented, depending on the illusion that his characters have his own gift of utterance in which to express themselves, with almost never an unfinished or broken speech among them, and yet still within their own personal idiom), then we can hear and recognize them.

If you use no slang, you will also be able to be translated more easily. If your characters use phrases like "old bean," or "wizard" as an adjective, or refer to a woman as a "dame, broad, doll, tomato or chippy," it will be hard for the translator to find the exact equivalent in another language to produce the same effect. I wonder if any of us know how much we lose in translations. Quite apart from the actual idiom (and I do not know how much foreign playwrights employ that), there is still the sound of the author's own voice, the quality of his personal style, which can never be put across in translation. We are reduced to a somewhat bare summary of the play and its conversation. Or, at least, we may be. I do not know.

Granville Barker made a translation, or a paraphrase, of Schnitzler's *Anatol* which was enchanting. He turned it into a personal and idiomatic English, which meant, I am sure, that he took a great many liberties with the original. As he himself was a major playwright of great taste, this seemed to me a highly proper thing to do, and I asked him, on the only occasion that I met him, why he did not do the same thing for Ibsen. He himself had had great success as an Ibsen director, but he must have suffered from those formidable, sometimes unspeakable, translations which are all that there are. Barker's answer was that it would not be possible with Ibsen, and that the gritty, stony, hard-on-the-feet English of the recognized translations was the best equivalent of Ibsen's own style. I could not answer this, because—knowing no Norwegian—I do not know Ibsen's own style. I have wondered about it ever since. I have seen one and read another of Ibsen's plays, retranslated. Madame Paxinou's *Hedda Gabler* had been retranslated by Ethel Borden and Mary Cass Canfield. These ladies knew no Norwegian, either. They had, however, secured a Norwegian friend who spoke both languages, and had got her to translate every line for them, and had, then, themselves, reproduced its effect in what sounded like contemporary stage English. To me, the result was fairly successful. They dodged a number of things that had become almost jokes in the better-known translations. "Fancy that, Hedda" had become "Can you imagine?" It sounded better to my ears, certainly better over Hedda's corpse. A number of the critics, however, objected to it. I think those critics were behaving a little like my mother when she objected to my own earlier dialogue. They were used to the old way. I thought, then, that Barker had been wrong.

But a year or two later, I read a new translation of *The Wild Duck* by James Bridie. Bridie also knew no Norwegian; he had gone to one of the traditional translations, and had reworded it himself. Now Bridie was one of the finest masters of dialogue that I know, but in this version of the Ibsen play, he went overboard. He used modern slang, he had Hedvig refer to her father as being "in awfully good form." The whole play became false in another way. It seemed to be moving in two worlds at once, and to be sure of itself in neither. Perhaps Barker was right. I wish that I knew Norwegian, myself.

Whether Ibsen generally wrote in the vernacular or not, I do not know, but here and there he does do so. Gina in *The Wild Duck* makes a couple of mistakes to prove that she is of an uneducated class. These mistakes have been translated into the word "pigstol" for "pistol," and "bemuse" for "amuse." These will not do at all. No uneducated woman has heard of the word "bemuse," and almost no uneducated woman will make a mistake on "amuse." The translator should have made an effort to find something more suitable. But the lines of dialogue referred to pistols and amusement. What was he to do? That is where local idiom can get in your way. I wonder how much we lose of

Chekhov? What we have is wonderful enough, but is there not perhaps much, much more buried in the quality of the lines, the tone of Chekhov's own voice? It is a sad thought. And no one is ever going to know for sure until a playwright comes along who knows Russian with absolute fluency, the fluency of having grown up with it as a language of his own, and a total command of dialogue in English, too. Those playwrights are very hard to find.

A lot of this is what must have been in my mother's mind when she criticized my dialogue, that it did not conform to the kind of dialogue that she was used to. But the dialogue in itself was not good. I know that. How was it bad? I have unfortunately no specimens of the period to look at. My earliest scraps of plays and of first acts left abandoned have vanished. But I think I know. I had developed no tone of voice of my own, only a scratchy and effortful method of speech, that was not unlike starting to talk in a foreign language. I did not know how speech should lead into speech, drawing the play with it. I devised little gimmicks, such as returning a borrowed book to explain a character's entrance, and then never went on with it. Perhaps I tried a comment on the borrowed book, something remembered from what an aunt of mine had once said, perhaps I actually made a joke, but it died there. I never let the book have its own tiny part in the story, never led the conversation from the book and through the book into the channels where I had to go. I finished with the book, and then said, "By the way," to start on the next track. I was always using "By the way." I added jokes where I could think of them, then I went into plain plot narration. I let my characters wallow in self-pity and self-analysis, flatly laid out to say the things I needed said. I covered nothing, doubled nothing, characterized nothing. And I had no ear, no ear at all, it seems to me now.

The ear is an essential quality of the dialogue-writer, the ear that can catch and reproduce the tone of characters' speech. I showed some sign of it in the first play that I have already outlined, because I was writing of people that I knew. I was not trying to be dramatic and theatrical about them, I was trying merely to put them on the stage. And when I did know them, they happened. They talked like real people, sometimes a little too much like real people, without selectiveness, repetitively, weakly, a little too much like ordinary people's chatter. That is something else to be learned. Really good dialogue is not what it would be in life; it can only seem to sound as if it were. No stage bore can be boring in the way a real life bore is. He would bore the audience, too. Look at the characters in C. K. Munro's play, *At Mrs. Beam's,* for this. They are all boardinghouse bores. There are moments, when they go on too long, when they seem almost to be bores, themselves, but for the most part they are brilliantly entertaining. I could never have achieved that then, even though we had lived in a boardinghouse where all the characters were C. K. Munro people. I had not yet learned how to select and how to seem to reproduce.

Take these lines of Miss Shoe in that play—I am going to have to do a little quoting in these chapters. She is talking to Laura, the adventuress.

MISS SHOE
Let me see, Rio? Oh, that's in Brazil, isn't it? Well, now, tell me about it. Is it pleasant there? I think it must be very pleasant.

LAURA
Oh, it's much like other places, I think.

MISS SHOE

Oh, but my dear, it must, I think, be quite delightful. I know I used to know a friend many years ago, who'd been in Rio, and she used to tell me about it. The great river with all the shipping on it, miles of wharves, and then further up the wonderful jungles and forests, through which the river finds its way. Oh yes, she told me about it, and you must tell me about it. Yes, Brazil must be a wonderful country—quite impenetrable in parts, quite impenetrable. Have you ever been in those parts?

LAURA

In—?

MISS SHOE

In the impenetrable parts, you know; where man can penetrate no farther owing to the thickness of the jungle and the feverish character of the swamps?

LAURA

No, I don't think I was ever in those parts.

MISS SHOE

And a wonderful people, too—a daring, bold people, those adventurers must have been who sailed away into the West. I always feel a sort of fellow-feeling with them, because I feel that that's just the sort of thing I should have liked to do, had things been otherwise. I suppose it's because I come of many races. I have cosmopolitan blood in me.

This is a tiny fragment of Miss Shoe only. She goes on and on like that for pages, but she amuses us because she is like Jane Austen's Miss Bates, she can dive downward into an endless fountain of self-revealing speech. "The impenetrable parts, where man can penetrate no further," what a quality of second-hand romanticism that calls up, derived from books on travel. Laura's answer is a surprising laugh in the theater, too. It marks the joke for us, in its vague helplessness under the flow of chatter. That is the kind of thing that I would have loved to be able to do over my aunts, and the boardinghouse people I had met. I could not do it, because I had never listened acutely, had listened only for the easy jokes, and had never got inside the people, had never understood them as they saw themselves, and also because I did not know, quite apart from mere reproduction, how and what to select.

There are briefer ways of doing it. Granville Barker showed that in the first act of *The Madras House*. I have just reread that act, looking for a passage to quote from it. I cannot find any, without wanting to go on and copy out the entire act. I think that is a good thing. The entire act moves almost uncuttably from start to finish. I think it was this act which did more for me as a young playwright than any other piece of dramatic literature. It tells very little in the way of plot, but it describes in the exactest detail the hour before lunch on a Sunday morning in a middle-class London suburban household. I knew those hours very well. I had spent many of them in my grandmother's house, when the uncles and aunts had come to call. Barker showed me that they could be put on the stage. In that first act, he introduces eleven characters, and makes most of them swiftly and superbly vivid. They include the five unmarriageable Huxtable daughters. I do not say that he distinguishes these from each other, but that was not his purpose. He selects one only, and leaves the rest in a lump, to illustrate that purpose, which was to show the horror of those girls who knew, almost for a certainty, that they would never get married, living under the same roof as their parents. Their indistinguishability is essential to their existence. They all have small remarks of equal tepidity. Even their father cannot quite remember them apart, introducing the same one a second time. The chain of hellos and good-byes, the opening greeting by each one as she appears: "Well, what a surprise. Will you stay to dinner?"—these are the things that seemed miraculous to me as a playwright then. I knew them all in life, could I reproduce them in the theater? If so, then I could be a playwright, too, perhaps. I knew that I could never think of the strong plots that Pinero invented, or the wordage for the big dialogue scenes—but the domestic detail, the creation of real people whom I was meeting, that perhaps I could manage. That was what I wanted to manage.

I became a playwright, I think, at a rather special and, for me, a valuable moment, just as I think that younger playwrights today in America may be hitting another moment of value, another slight turning point in the drama. When I began to write plays, it was just after the First World War. The theater was turning then from the more dramatic vehicles of plot, and the plays in which characters usually had titles, to a more local, more domestic kind of drama, where the people were more ordinary, more like my own family and friends, more like the people I knew and could observe and report on. The theater having always had a deep fascination for me, I was grateful and eager to practice in this newer, more familiar kind. I had a great deal to learn, and the first and most important thing was to manage dialogue. I had to learn that there was a great deal more to it than mere reportage, but perhaps that had to come first.

CHAPTER ELEVEN

Dialogue—II

I WENT ON trying to write plays, and as I wrote about the things that I knew, the dialogue became better. My ear was getting trained. When I wrote about the things that I did not know, and when I tried to make jokes, it stayed bad. I have just reread the plays that I wrote immediately before *Young Wood-ley*. The dialogue is strengthening in them, there is a little more cohesion to it. Most of the people talk like people, although they still have the tendency to expatiate about themselves, and there is a good deal of flatness still around. *Young Woodley*, written when I was twenty-four, is an extraordinary improvement. The difference between it and the play I wrote three months earlier is hard to believe. Oddly (and this is something that can often happen, and young playwrights had better be warned about it), the two plays that followed it seem to me now a great deal less good. I had gone back to some of my older and some of my trickier habits of dialogue. The step forward and

138

the subsequent step backward are of oddly frequent occurrence. I do not know why they should be, but I can also encourage the younger writer by assuring him that the step forward is almost never made on its own. It will claim its own permanent ground before very long.

I do not think that *Young Woodley* was as good as was then claimed for it, but I think it was surprising for me. I think the boys are well written. There again I was writing something that I knew, and doing a good and selective job of representation. My ear had heard them well. For all that a critic (who is a good friend of mine, and has no more forgotten his remark now, after twenty-five years, than I have) said that the sex talk was "awkward and inhibited," I do not think it was, by the stage standard of those days. The fact that the Censor banned the play in England (and that my mother was shocked by it) seems to me some proof to the contrary. I think I managed the father well; he still sounds real and vivid to me. I failed, I think, with the schoolmaster and his wife, partly, as I have said, because I hated and loved them too much, and also because they were drawn more from fiction than from life. Laura suggests the woman who talks of her books, her flowers and her music, and she has a maddening kind of nobility about her. I was doing some literary writing here, too, with her speeches about education and young people. I would warn all writers against speeches that deal with life in general, and with the principles and lessons one can learn from it. Generalizations about life make for bad writing. They are the author speaking, the author rubbing it in. They are only one degree removed from the long speech that starts with: "Let me tell you a little about marriage."

After another couple of plays, I wrote *After All,* another

domestic piece, and here I achieved most of what I was after. The detail was there, plenty of it, but it was selective and accurate now. The dialogue had hardened into good dialogue. I have used that phrase already, but I have not yet explained what I mean by it. I mean, first, that it had attained its own speed, that the scenes were of the right length, the speeches of the right length, and for the most part nothing dragged or dawdled. Speed is an important thing. Every playwright has his own speed, and mine is slower than I wish it were. There are slower writers still. George Kelly is one of the slowest. When I saw *Daisy Mayme* on my first visit to America, I was amazed at the time it took over almost nothing. Here is a short passage from its first act.

AUNT OLLY
[Played by Miss Josephine Hull]
I think you're a little thinner, Ruth.

RUTH
Oh, no such luck, Aunt Olly, I'm getting stouter by the minute.

OLLY
You look thinner to me, dear.

RUTH
Well, it must be the black, for I weigh a hundred and twenty-two pounds.

OLLY
Do you really weigh that much, Ruth?

RUTH
A hundred and twenty-two pounds. I was weighed two weeks ago.

MRS. FENNER
(*Ruth's mother*)
You must have lost a few of those pounds today, didn't you, Ruth?

RUTH

I hope so. Isn't that terrible?

OLLY

Why, that's three pounds more than I weigh, dear.

RUTH

Do you only weigh a hundred and nineteen pounds, Aunt Olly?

OLLY

That's what I weighed the last time I was weighed.

MRS. FENNER

Well, it must have been a long time ago, Olly.

OLLY

It couldn't have been such a very long time ago, Laura, for it was down at Doctor DeShanty's, and I've only been going to him since November.

MRS. FENNER

Well, I don't think you could have had both feet on the scale, if you only weighed a hundred and nineteen pounds.

The scene about the weighing actually goes on longer than this, but that is its speed of writing, and as I listened to it, it seemed to me to be moving even slower than *At Mrs. Beam's*. I can remember thinking that I would not be able to bear it, and then as the performance moved on, it had established the tempo for the whole play. The characters became endearing, because one knew them so well, and the whole *rallentando* speed of the play was essential to its mood. All the same, I would advise a younger playwright to beware of George Kelly until his own speed had become set for him first.

A slightly similar mood, keyed to a sharper, though still gentle mood of comedy, comes from Paul Osborn's enchanting *Morning's at Seven*. Here the reluctant forty-year-old Homer, his fiancée, Myrtle, aged thirty-nine, and his mother are sitting together in the back yard.

MYRTLE

I love your back yard, Mrs. Bolton. It looks so cool. It's simply heavenly.

IDA

Yes, we like it very much.

MYRTLE

All the trees and everything. I bet you sit out here all the time.

IDA

We sit out here a good deal of the time.

MYRTLE

Well, I should think you would. It's simply heavenly. I don't know when I've seen a more attractive back yard.

IDA

Yes, we're very fond of it.

MYRTLE

Well, I should think so. It's so nice and wild, too. Like being in a forest.

IDA

I'm glad you like it.

MYRTLE

Well, I certainly do. It's simply—heavenly, that's all there is to it.

IDA

Well, it's nice of you to say so.

MYRTLE

Well, I mean it.

HOMER

Have mosquitoes sometimes.

IDA

Yes, there are mosquitoes sometimes.

MYRTLE

How dreadful!

IDA

But I don't think we've had quite so many this year as usual. Have you noticed that, Homer?

HOMER

Not so many. That's right.

MYRTLE

Isn't that interesting the way those things go? One year you'll have a lot of mosquitoes and the next year not so many mosquitoes. Or a lot of caterpillars one year and the next year not so many caterpillars. I wonder why that is.

IDA

I don't know why that is. Do you, Homer?

HOMER

No, I don't know why that is.

MYRTLE

It's very interesting, isn't it? Anyway I suppose the mosquitoes and the caterpillars and all those things have some purpose. They wouldn't have been put there if they hadn't.

IDA

No, I don't suppose they would have.

HOMER

Don't suppose so.

MYRTLE

It's all a part of some big plan. Some big—plan of some kind.

This is slow playwriting, too, but it is exquisite. The repeat of the word "heavenly" is like a delicious chime. Notice, too, that neither George Kelly, nor Paul Osborn, nor C. K. Munro in the passage from *At Mrs. Beam's* is disliking his characters or poking malicious fun at them. They can see their humor, but they see it with a loving tenderness. That is why the scenes are so good. It would have been easy to exaggerate Aunt Olly or Myrtle, and the resulting laughs would have been bigger, but the gentleness and the reality of the scenes would have gone. The play would have been nearer to a cheaper kind of farce.

On the other side of the ledger, there are the fast-moving playwrights. This is not a question of the length of the speeches. Noel Coward started the vogue for brief speeches, almost none more than a line long, in the mid-twenties, but for all that the rate of speed is not necessarily increased. The brief speeches can dawdle as much as the longer ones, like Miss Shoe's. The speeches in *Daisy Mayme,* quoted above, are all brief ones, but the play idles its way as though it were all on a long summer afternoon. It is a frame of mind, a speed of mind. No one illustrates this better, I think, than James Bridie. I have searched a shelf of his plays this morning, hunting for the right passage to quote, and have found myself reading him for several hours, unable to put a book down. The trouble has been to find an isolated scene that will give the quality I want to illustrate. I have chosen a scene from *The King of Nowhere*. It is not the best, it is not Bridie's writing at its most dazzling, but I think it gives an idea of his vitality. A doctor is seated waiting. He has been called in to certify Frank Vivaldi, a great and popular actor, as insane. Vivaldi enters. He is normally dressed, but he wears the make-up of a Pierrot, which is the part he is currently playing.

VIVALDI

Hello! What's this? Who are you?

MCGILP

I am Doctor McGilp.

VIVALDI

Never heard of you.

MCGILP

I know that. Dr. Wanstead asked me to call on you.

VIVALDI

Why? I didn't authorize that.

MCGILP

He said you weren't very fit.

VIVALDI

I never felt fitter in my life.

MCGILP

I'm glad to hear that. Had you a good house to-night?

VIVALDI

No. Lousy. Packed like sardines in a tin, of course. And oily like sardines, and smelly like sardines; and no heads, like sardines.

MCGILP

Not sympathetic?

VIVALDI

Who wants an audience to be sympathetic? Only an artist can be sympathetic towards an artist. But I need something to work on. A little intelligence. Only a little.

MCGILP

Perhaps it's because you're a little nervy. . . .

VIVALDI

No. But I'm rather tired. So perhaps you'll excuse me. . . .

MCGILP

It must be an appalling strain to lift a heavy audience, especially when you have other worries. . . .

VIVALDI

It is indeed. It's a vile life, an actor's. . . . I lifted them, though, I lifted them.

(*Suddenly*)

Who told you I had other worries?

MCGILP

I can see that you have. I'm a doctor.

VIVALDI

You can't see my face.

MCGILP

I can see your hands.

VIVALDI

Why haven't you mentioned my face? Are you trying to humour me?

MCGILP

I only humour fools. And not many of them. Is that how you paint your face in the play?

VIVALDI

Yes. Haven't you seen the play?

MCGILP

No. Why didn't you take off your make-up?

VIVALDI

I had a particular reason for that.

MCGILP

What was your reason?

VIVALDI

Do you mind if we don't discuss that? If you want to see my face, there it is.

(*He hands a photograph*)

That's my Hamlet. Have you seen it?

MCGILP

No. But it is very like Hamlet.

VIVALDI

You think so? You've read the play?

McGILP

Yes. I've read the play. That's Hamlet's face all right.

VIVALDI

As you imagined it?

McGILP

Yes. It's the face of a man with bad dreams.

VIVALDI

Yes. But I hadn't bad dreams, then.

McGILP

You have them now?

VIVALDI

Yes. I wish the doctors could do something to . . . oh, well, it doesn't matter.

McGILP

It does matter. I've come here to help you. Why don't you tell me what's troubling you?

VIVALDI

If they would only let me alone. If they would only let me alone. I've done them no harm. Why should I have to slink and hide and disguise myself?

McGILP

Don't you think you had better let me have the whole story?

VIVALDI

You look as if I could trust you. You look like an eagle.

McGILP

Go on. What's troubling you?

VIVALDI

It sounds foolish. It sounds almost—
(*He laughs*)

—almost mad. But there's a big conspiracy, and I've fallen foul of it somehow. They've agents watching me day and night. Not in the theatre, though. Not in front. They're too clever for that. But they wait for me at the stage-door. They follow me back here. If I look round and face them, they get out of sight. Gosh, they had better! I've had about enough of them. I found out to-night a way to prevent them following me. I don't know how long it will work. I thought, "It's the make-up that saves me in the theatre. I'm all right so long as I'm somebody else." So I kept this on. It's all right so far.

That scene takes place within five minutes of the rise of the curtain. You could imagine its being sufficient to last as an opening for the rest of the play. It does not. It is an introductory scene, a prologue. The play starts five minutes later, in an entirely different setting on the Scottish moors, with some fascinating and entirely new people, drawn with a speed and a vitality that are exciting. Presently, Vivaldi appears, having escaped from the lunatic asylum. The lady who owns the house has the idea of making him a great public leader. From there, the play goes forward, and at a rate that stops you from even noticing the pages turning, until its last act, where they become suddenly weighted.

I would like to take a few moments on James Bridie. There is a lot to be learned from him. He is not well-known in America. He had a few plays produced here, and none of them were successes. He never stopped having plays produced in England. A great many of them were failures there, too, but they were a different kind of failure, a more noticed failure, and there were a number of big successes. He was a Scottish doctor, and he wrote his plays—an enormous number of them—in his spare time. He was a lazy playwright. He would never take the job quite seriously, and he wrote his plays as though they were pieces for amateur productions. His last acts almost always go to pieces. He had genius, and I make no bones about using that word, but it was a careless genius, and had nothing to do with taking pains. There was an afternoon when I was in Glasgow, where he lived, and I was complaining that there was no theater for me to go to that night. He suggested I go to a company of Yiddish players. I replied that I had outgrown the belief that one could go to a play in a totally foreign language and find the acting so wonderful that it did not matter that one had no idea what the play was all about. At best, I said, after you have carefully read the plot on the program, you will know only when the play is being funny and when it is being sad. "My dear boy," replied Bridie, "that's all that audiences know of us at any time." That remark, I think, betokened his own attitude to the theater, and perhaps to his audience. Playwriting was a pastime with him, and I was never sure that he had any respect for his public. If I had asked him why he was able to write such enchanting and humorous dialogue, he would have replied that he did it to amuse himself. The theater may be a perishable and ephemeral commodity, but I do not think it should be quite as ephemeral as all that.

Bridie's genius consisted in being able to create an endless supply of new and arresting characters. They were real people, and one felt one had never seen them on the stage before. He could bring them alive in four sentences. He had a tremendous sweep. He could create a sense of the vastness of life, both inside and outside his play. There were always larger interests outside the windows, threatening to break in. He could include a wonderful panorama of past and present, so that in *A Sleeping Clergyman* he seemed to me to be presenting a great colonnade of huge arches opening backward into eternity, with the great chords of music, such as E. M. Forster heard in *War and Peace,* accompanying it. He made me feel a sissy as a playwright. He could make me laugh and he could make me cry. He could do everything, except write a totally good play. He was the most fascinating, and the most maddening playwright of my lifetime. There is a great deal to be learned from him, and a great deal to be copied—if you can do it.

There are other points to dialogue that arise from this question of speed. These will depend on an author's ear, a knowledge of when to increase and when to decrease the speed of writing, which scene needs to move fast and which must be slowed down. This is akin to a director's sense of tempo in playing a scene. It will come from practice and from the practiced ear. An author, having written his scene, will do well to read it aloud, to try and hear it in a theater, even to try and direct it in his head so that it will be a simple and not a complicated thing for the real director when he comes to it. Never rely on your director to pull you out of your trouble. There is the knowledge, too, of how long a scene should take. This knowledge also is instinctive, and it cannot be solved by listing the number of pages in advance, though that may be of help. Every playwright has an idea of how long he thinks he will need, but every scene takes its own time when you come to write it. A five-page scene can suddenly reduce itself to two, and a two-page scene can run itself to six. The word "Curtain" can suddenly jump out at you, or it can hold itself off. You will learn as you write whether or not your scenes will hold as you have written them and you will learn better as you see them rehearsed and played. That is one of the main reasons for playing out of town. The audience reaction may not tell you much that is of value, and it can tell you things that are of harm to you, but your own sense, if you have developed it, will tell you about the length of your scenes. Howard Lindsay has said, and very rightly, that a couple of lines can make a scene too long, four lines make it very much too long, and six can make it impossible. You would not have thought that cutting four lines out of a scene can make much difference. I have done it, and I know it can. You will listen, and you will listen night after night, and you will find the lines in which the scene seems suddenly to repeat itself, to add unnecessarily to itself, to overstrengthen a point already clearly made. You may not hear the audience shuffling or coughing, but you can feel it getting ready to do so. Then cut, cut until it has got your point and has no time to realize that it has.

Cutting, and a willingness to cut, are two things that can serve a playwright best. The younger the author, the more likely he is to fall in love with his dialogue, and to be unwilling to part with a line of it. As he grows up, he will learn that there is always going to be room elsewhere for more, and be willing even to sacrifice jokes, jokes that he cannot put into other plays because they sprang from the characters and situations in this play, if he sees or is shown that he must. He will learn to shrug his shoulders with the knowledge that there are as good fish in the sea as ever came out of it. (I think when he grows really old, the youthful infatuation returns again, as a sign of senility.) It is essential that he should achieve this. Few plays have been damaged by cutting, and most have been improved. I am talking now of cutting not only lines, but also words. You will find that words produce a rhythm of their own, and they can delay and flatten out a scene. The "Well" and "Yes, but" that start almost every other speech can hold up a manuscript, as can the repetition of "I think" and "I believe." They can also weaken the character that speaks them, and they can end by becoming a personal and irritating habit of the author's, started once to try to break down the set speeches of an earlier type of dialogue and turn it into a nearer kind of vernacular, ending now by reducing it to a tepid form of chatter.

There is another point about dialogue, good dialogue, which is an essential one that I am always having to relearn and remember. This is that a scene must always make a straight line, develop its thought and its purpose on a straight line, without byways. It is a bad fault of mine to forget this. I start a scene to prove or discuss one thing, find another point springing from the dialogue, follow that new point to its conclusion, and then have to go back and pick up the original idea, very often with a "By the way" to bring it back to hand. Watch out for that "By the way," or "As we were saying." I have had to rewrite several of my better scenes in rehearsal for this reason, and I have had to rearrange much of the material in this book for the same one. I cannot give you scene examples, because I never keep first drafts, but I know the practice well, and I know that it is fatal. Watch your scenes, see that they go to their main point in one direct line. If the subsidiary point is an interesting one, then take it first or take it later, but never interject it. You will lose your flow, your main point and the attention of your audience, if you do.

Your audience has learned a kind of shorthand in the theater, a shorthand by which it picks up what you are trying to convey. But because it is a shorthand, it may also pick up more than you meant it to. You must learn the shorthand with it. One bitter or unsympathetic remark from a character can stamp that character as unattractive to the audience so that there is no possibility for him to escape that impression thereafter. To you, the author, the remark may well have been uttered as such remarks are in life, as one among many brought out in a moment of irritation. The remark is real and true, it would have been said, but it can do you harm that you never expected. You can wreck a whole stage marriage by just that. The same is true of business, whether you write it or whether the director incorporates it. A moment or two of tidying the room, and the character is set as fussy or house-proud for you. A refusal of a drink can make them careful as to their consumption, and two refusals can make them permanent teetotalers. These are all part of the shorthand, and they are things to watch. Almost no line or action can be there for no purpose at all. The audience will store it away as squirrels store nuts, and it can later be brought out and thrown at you. It can even provide a wrong laugh for you.

Laughter in the theater, the right laughter, is one of the happiest sounds in an author's life. It springs best from his own viewpoint, his own absorption in his characters and their situations. The days of epigrams are past; lines that are funny on their own are rare; humor comes most easily from the author's own mood, and from his people. The beginner has always the idea that in a comedy every line must be a bright one, and every answer a crack. That is not true. Do not think you must be funny every line. Actually, anyway, you cannot. Almost every speech, of no matter what length, has room for only a certain number of laughs in it. An actress pointed this out to me once, and I think that she was right. Try to add to the laughs with a new joke that you have just thought of, and one of the old ones will fail, to make room for it. Remember, too, that every laugh needs a moment or two to recover from it. Two jokes in successive lines can kill each other. The second one will not be properly heard. Your jokes must be spaced, carefully spaced. Nor can they be inserted, just as such. A notebook is of little use to you. You will merely find yourself wasting half a page of time to drag in some remark that you have jotted down. The best laughs come from character, from the reaction of a character to a situation. That is why you can so seldom quote them; the characters and the situation have to be there first.

Family jokes, personal jokes, are almost always untransferable. Dodie Smith knew this in her play *Dear Octopus*. She needed a reference to a family joke in order to relate its members, and to isolate the one outside, but she knew enough, too, not to explain it. "Never try to explain a family joke, Mother," the son remarks, "they sound the merest gibberish." Purely verbal jokes, sophisticated puns and plays on words are seldom as good in the theater as they look on paper. The late Philip Barry was greatly given to these. They always amused me, because my own sense of humor is largely a verbal one, but the critics have never seemed to care about them. The young man in *Without Love* who, when he hears that someone has given his girl orchids from the White House greenhouse, starts to quote: "Snitched them from the White House greenhouse. Wear them with the fur-side outside. Wear them with the skin-side inside. Daughter of the wind, Nokomis," delighted me as I am sure that he delighted Philip Barry. I never saw the play performed, and I do not know how the joke got over, but I know that his puns did not always do so. The young man who had been "faithful to thee after my old-fashioneds," and the lady who was feeling "ept and ert," a play on the words "inept and inert"; these denote a very personal kind of wit, and a personal preference. They are apt to irritate audiences, and to sound a little like an uncle at the family dinner table.

In finishing up with the subject of dialogue, look back for a moment at the lines you remember best from plays, and see what they are. A few of them will be lines essential to the theme of the play, like the line in *Death of a Salesman* about the boy who is liked, but not well liked. The theme of the play is in that line, as it is in the line about salesmen "out there in the blue, riding on a smile and a shoeshine." These lines are best when they spring from the character who makes them, said in his voice, and are not the superimposed voice of the author talking to his audience. That is one of the great dangers of the propaganda plays, plays with a social message; the author talks too much in them. Howard Lindsay has said that if you are going to write a propaganda play, do not let any character in the play know what the propaganda is. I would add to that, never let anyone but the characters do the talking, and never let any character represent yourself.

Oddly, however, I think the lines that you will remember best are the characters' own unconscious definitions of themselves, their small revealing comments on life. Again in the *Salesman,* a well-remembered line is Willy Loman's flash-back to something his wife said earlier about the whipped cheese that she has bought. Willy is ranting about the state of the world, and then breaks off suddenly to say, apropos of nothing: "How can they whip cheese?" There are remarks of this kind in *The Glass*

Menagerie—Amanda's speeches about chewing food, and about the jonquils; Laura's line about having been called "blue roses" because she had said she had pleurosis—and from *A Streetcar Named Desire,* there are Stanley's lines about his acquaintances who deal with women's dresses and jewelry and law whom he will call in to handle these things for him, and almost every line of Blanche's self-dramatizations. Her line about Poe, corrected to Mr. Edgar Allan Poe, will always ring in my head. These are lines that create people and their backgrounds, that reveal a little more than they meant them to. The aunt in my own play who did not want a cocktail, but would have the cherry if there was one, is perhaps another example. She was the wife of a provincial college professor, and when she hears of the famous playwright whose son she has just met, she adds: "I acted in one of his father's plays two Christmases ago, when the College staff did it for the Infirmary." Her more sophisticated sister replies: "Your life's one continual round of gaiety, isn't it, Nellie dear?" These lines created Nellie's background, and they also established, I think, the difference between the two sisters, and the slight heartlessness of the older one who can snub her like that.

There are the endearing lines, too, that the character is not aware of, but which make us love him. There is the hero's line in *All My Sons* where, after he has embraced the girl he has always loved, he draws back and says with a kind of wondering amazement: "God, I kissed you, Annie. I kissed Annie." I have not forgotten that instant which communicated to me all that the rather rough young man was feeling within himself. There is a minor and tiny line in *Point of No Return* which has great charm for me. The young man on the train is talking to the hero about

New York and his last visit there. "We sure had a time," he says. "We took New York apart." And then, after a commendatory "Yeah" from the hero, he adds: "We didn't really take it apart. We got awfully drunk, though." In that moment, I loved the character for his awareness of what he had said, of the Rotarian sound of the boast that he had just made, and for the modest knowledge that his behavior had been small and ordinary. He became a very endearing person to me. It could have taken pages to make him that with a narration of his circumstances in life. The line did it, instantaneously.

There are even lesser touches than these, the tiny choice of words, of habits of speech that can identify a character. I would exemplify these with the "Oh, my" exclamations from the father in *Point of No Return,* which are peculiarly revealing of a personality, and those of an elderly, fussy and benevolent gentleman, for whom in *Somebody Knows* I invented a trick of repeating the same words or thoughts followed by "indeed." He is having tea with an old lady, and praising her cake to her. "Rich and rare, Madame. Rich and rare. A very succulent cake, indeed." "Rich and rare" as applied to a homemade cake had been spoken first by our family doctor when I was a small boy. It had lingered in my mind for over thirty years before it cropped up again here. Those are some of the ways in which dialogue is fashioned. Memory plays a large part, too. Yet all of these can be used sparingly only. They can be employed only to indicate a character, never to create one. They can never be used to excess, or they become the typical phrase, like Mrs. Micawber's determination never to desert Mr. Micawber, or Mrs. Gummidge's capacity to "feel things more," and produce what E. M. Forster called the "flat" character, which can never be caught or seen in the round. No author should feel that every line of a character's dialogue must be marked with these phrases, nor work too hard for this kind of verbal coloring, trying to employ it all the time.

The above are details, though they are important. There are other lines that are better than details. Occasionally in life, and still more occasionally in plays, people will quite unconsciously deliver themselves of a line that reveals them wholly and forever. It is almost as though a butterfly had impaled itself on a pin, and had then put a label beneath itself on a piece of paper. The instances of this in drama are rare, but when they occur they are wonderful. I have searched my memory for an example. I can think of none better than in the last act of *Hedda Gabler* where, after Eilert's death, Tesman and Mrs. Elvsted sit down to try and reconstruct his manuscript. Hedda wanders in on them, asks how they are getting on. "It will be terribly hard to put in order," says Mrs. Elvsted. "We must manage it," Tesman replies. "I am determined." And then he adds the miraculous line: "Arranging other people's papers is just the work for me." He has no idea what he has done for himself in saying that, but the butterfly has impaled itself, has labeled itself as the man with no creative edge or ability of his own, and no longing for it, but who feels that he is truly fulfilling himself when he is putting someone else's work in order. We know him, we understand him forever, and we know Hedda, too, the emptiness and contempt of her marriage, her whole appreciation of Tesman and the futility of everything that lies before her. There is a lesser example in *The Wild Duck*. I became aware of it at a London production, having missed its subtlety in reading the play. It comes where Hedvig is explaining how she learned to pray, when her father was ill with "leeches on his neck, and said that death was staring him in the face." This line is a revelation of Hjalmar and all his self-dramatization, though Hedvig has taken him with deep seriousness. Over and over again, Ibsen proved his genius in this way. These lines, I would say, never come from thought on the part of the dramatist, any more than they do from the person who makes them in real life. They are gifts from the subconscious, straight gifts from God.

Lastly, I would say one more thing. There is a test for good dialogue. Do you have to look and see who is speaking? In plays typed as they are in England, the names of the characters are put at the side, instead of above the spoken line. Quite often, the manuscripts are bound too close to the side, and in reading them it becomes necessary to pull the cover back to see the name of the speaker. If, after a page or two, you no longer have to do this, if you know who is speaking from the tone of the voice, then the author has done a good job. And he can do this and still retain the sound of his own voice as well, as a good mimic can imitate the voices of several people, and yet have his own personal quality identifiable, too. Perhaps dialogue-writing is only a form of mimicry, of hearing and copying and reproducing, but remember, too, that there are all kinds of mimics. Most of them write their own material, and most of their material is poor rather than good. They select what qualities they are going to use to bring the mimickee before us; if they are good mimics, they select qualities that other mimics of the same person have left out. There is a quality of fine dramatic criticism in the best mimicry, a comment on the person imitated, sometimes praise, sometimes blame. A good mimic has a great deal to commend him. So has the good writer of dialogue.

CHAPTER TWELVE

Holding the Audience

WHAT KIND of play is it that you are going to write? There used to be more labels for plays than there would seem to be a use for nowadays. My father used to like two kinds—what he called the strong play and the human play. I always had the idea that a strong play was a little like cheese, and could be too strong for some tastes. I am not sure that I was not right. The strong play was grim, aiming at a subject not popular with audiences, tabooing attempts at theatrical effectiveness, and often ending in suicide. Plays like *Rutherford and Son*, about a stern and unforgiving business father; Galsworthy's *Strife*, which was about strikes; and *Hindle Wakes*, about an equality of sex rights for men and women; these were strong plays. It was their conscious strength that made them inoffensive if their subjects were dubious. Lillian Hellman writes strong plays today, and so does Arthur Miller. It used not to be a successful kind of play, but times and appetites are chang-

ing, and I have not heard the word "strong" in that connection
for a good many years. Human plays were about a rather sacrificial and especially forgiving type of love, and they touched an
audience to tears. These are, I think, what C. E. Montague
described as "Unwholesome and Wholesome Plays," a description which was not without a touch of malice.

There were also problem plays. I can remember the term very
clearly. They were usually about whether a husband should for-
give a wife under such and such circumstances, or whether a
wife ought to tell. You do not need to ask what she ought to tell;
it varied with the year. I cannot now remember having seen a
problem play, describable as such, for a great many years. A
few categories seem still to remain. Fantasies are still spoken
of as such, and there is a theory that they are dangerous; the
movies are sure that audiences do not like them. This would
seem a rather ridiculous theory when one remembers the successes of any of J. M. Barrie's pieces, of *Berkeley Square,* of
On Borrowed Time, of *Harvey* with its imaginary rabbit, of
Mrs. McThing, and even of my own *Bell, Book and Candle.* To
say nothing of those written by Thornton Wilder, which are
superb and stand all by themselves. It is true that a number of
people have a certain resistance to any fantastic idea, and to
being forced to make the jump with their imaginations, but
there do not seem to be enough of them to bother about. There
was also a kind of play that I do not think I have ever seen one
of—called an extravaganza. I would very much like to meet
one, any time. Perhaps *The Skin of Our Teeth* was that. If so,
I would like to see more of them.

But if the labels have fallen a good deal into desuetude, the
author himself must know what he is doing, what he is after,

what key he is trying to strike, and must stay within that key. He must remember the Unities. Comedy, farce, tragedy and melodrama all have different conventions, different moods, and the author must observe them. Every work of art, it has been said, must be judged by laws deducible from itself. The characters in farce are more improbable, more overdrawn, less realistic than they are in comedy, and so are the situations in which they are placed. Tragedy is grimmer than a straight drama, and usually shows it early in its presentation, if only by the stark forbidding of laughter. Playwrights today, however, are departing from this, and I think wisely. *Death of a Salesman* was a tragedy, and so, I think, was *A Streetcar Named Desire*, but the authors of those plays did not acknowledge that fact by the rock-bound sternness of their handling. Beware of the author who is too Greek from the beginning. An author's sense of universal timelessness, of a tragic applicability to all humanity, is dangerous to a script. As Walter Kerr, critic of the *Herald-Tribune*, has recently said, it too frequently involves a pause in the characters' humanity for station identification.

Melodrama is keyed more roughly than drama, and it can handle coincidence with a better digestion. The dramatic writer must avoid coincidence as a cheaper form of food, and if he uses it, is apt to apologize for it in his dialogue as a hostess is apt to apologize for serving hamburgers. I recently learned that the phrase "the long arm of coincidence" comes from a play by that almost wholly forgotten playwright, C. Haddon Chambers, author of *The Tyranny of Tears* and *Passers By*. If his pieces have ceased to be remembered, his phrase will last forever. Melodrama can handle that arm. It uses, too, less subtlety of character-drawing, paints itself in a stronger contrast of colors.

We still look for the bad man and the good girl in melodrama, and we are slightly pained when they vary from these degrees and become more complicated and more real. The plot instantly becomes less real to us.

But the author will set his mood for himself, feel it for himself, and stay within it. Technique is his means for the projection of that mood, and the handling of stage mechanism within it. There are a hundred illustrations of it, a thousand points to learn and to invent. The whole of William Archer's book on *Play-making* is devoted to the skill of craftsmanship. The only trouble with it is that, having been published in 1912, it seems now like a manual for the writing of plays that no one would want to go and see any more. But there are still many valuable tips to be found in it. This chapter, dealing with a few stage problems, will also be a chapter of tips. I know of no other way to present them.

There are many points that would seem too obvious to mention, yet I have seen them all ignored in the manuscripts of plays, many of which were by people one would have expected to know better. I can only assume that they were forgotten, that the authors forgot that they were writing for the theater. I have seen the playwright ask that meals should be served to a dozen or more people, with not more than a couple of lines to cover the serving. I have seen meals eaten, large meals, in a page of dialogue, by a character who talked almost the entire time. The playwright here has visualized nothing. His director will tell him, when they come to rehearsal, that these things are not possible, that to serve a dozen plates of spaghetti will take quite a while and there must be lines, a page of lines at least, to fill in that time. An audience will not watch a meal, unless it is an extremely meaningful one, being served in silence. The actors will show you, and very speedily, that they cannot eat and speak at the same moment. Their mouths will be full, and their words not heard. But it is better not to have to wait until rehearsal to learn these things. If you try to visualize your play being performed, you will not do them.

You must remember that costume-changing takes time, and you must allow for that time. If a scene curtain falls on your heroine in day clothes, and rises a half-minute later on her in evening dress, you will be in trouble. Do not think of her as "underdressing"; it is only a phrase you have heard. Such a thing is possible, especially with a skillful designer, but it should never be relied on. A change of costume takes anything from one to two minutes, and a page of dialogue can be estimated to last about a minute. Make your costume changes no less than that in length, and more if possible.

Never leave your stage completely empty. It can be done; it has been done very successfully in *Journey's End;* but it is a safer ruling that it will not work. The moment the stage is left bare, the audience's attention will start to wander, and will have to be recalled. I am always seeing stage directions in manuscripts where a character leaves the stage, and "after a moment" someone else walks on. The author again has not seen the play performed in his head, or stopped to wonder what will keep his audience's mind on the play during that moment he has so lightly described. It will seem not like a moment, but like a quarter of an hour. Similarly, it is unwise to leave a single character alone on the stage, unless he has some vital business to perform. Do not add that he will light a cigarette, pour himself a drink, or turn over the pages of an illustrated magazine. These things have no meaning; they are details that should fit into a scene as part of it; they cannot become a scene in themselves. Try always to arrange that the next character to appear shall do so before the departing character leaves the stage. It may mean a few extra lines of dialogue, and they may seem to you like waste dialogue, but they are better than that stage wait.

Never leave an important actor for long with nothing to say and nothing to do. Remember who is on stage, and keep them all in your scenes. An actor can listen for a while, if the scene is of importance to him and to his character, but he cannot stand or sit still with egg on his face. Balance your parts. Do not let a character start out importantly, as though he were to be one of the leading people, and then allow him to dwindle away. Alternatively, do not start with what looks like a lesser character, and then have it become a leading role later on. Do not dispense with your leading people, for the sake of a lesser story, late in the play. You will have created a main interest in your leads by then, and the audience will want to stay with it. If one of your leads is forced, by the circumstances of the plot, to be off stage for a long section of your last act, never let the audience forget him and his absence, but dramatize it through the other leading character as keenly as if he were there. If both your leading characters have to be absent, then I can only say that you have constructed your play wrong, and you are in the kind of trouble I predicted in the chapter about that.

Do not despise these things, nor leave them for your director to fix for you. It is his job to help you, but you cannot ask the impossible of him. Besides, he is not a playwright. He will know what can be done, and what cannot, but it is you who will have to find the remedies, and it is better that you should know the need for them in advance. A friend of Rupert Brooke's wrote that Brooke always spoke of poetry as though it were carpentering. All crafts are like that. Theatrical mechanics need as careful a manipulation of joins to make a steady and secure balance, and a removal of the signs of those joins, as does poetry or the making of a good chair. What I am saying now is a part of all that.

There is the question of stage time. What is the time limit for an act, how long a period can it seem to cover? It is always longer than the time of playing. (Remember, by the way, your playing time. With the ordinary stage typing, no act should be more than forty-eight pages nor less than thirty, I would say. Your last act should be your briefest. The total script should be not more than a hundred and twenty-five pages.) An act that covers forty-five pages can stretch itself to almost two hours of apparent time, if carefully handled. After that, you will have to drop the curtain to mark the passage of a longer period. You cannot have a character leave a house in Greenwich Village, go all the way to the Bronx and back, and return to the stage in the same act. The audience cannot be made to forget the distance. But you can make him go a good deal farther than would be truly possible in the ten minutes that he is off stage. It will depend on what you fill the intermediate scenes with. Chatter will not do. The audience will recognize it as such, and will know that it has covered no time at all. Vital action that catches its attention will cover a lot more time than it takes to play. The audience's interest has been diverted from your stagecraft. That is your main problem, here as elsewhere; never let the audience catch you at your tricks. And, therefore, be careful with such things as telling the audience the time, if it is important to you to

keep its mind off it. Do not let a character say: "How quick you
have been," if the person so addressed has really taken much
less time than he would actually have done. This is calling attention to it, reminding your audience of what it was essential to
you that it should avoid noticing.

Equally, never let a character say: "I don't know why I am
telling you all this." It is one of my unfavorite remarks in the
theater, and it can always tempt an audience to answer back:
"I don't, either." In England, restive audiences do answer back;
they shout things from the gallery. It is humiliating to the author, but it can teach him things, too. I am reminded here of
J. M. Barrie, who was usually a master of technique, in one of
his more recalcitrant moments. It is at the opening of Act Two of
Mary Rose. Some years have passed since Act One, and there is
a lot of exposition to be put over. Mary Rose runs on to the
Hebridean island on which the act is set. She throws her arms
around her old friend, a rowan tree and, being a Barrie heroine,
she bursts into reminiscent speech. She tells it she is married,
and for how long. Here, I feel that even Barrie's mind misgave
him. He heard that ugly fellow in the gallery calling out: "Go on,
give it all the news." And, as though to cover himself with that
interrupter, he hands that line to his hero. "Go on," he remarks,
"give it all the news. Tell it we don't have a house of our own
yet." And Mary Rose continues with her story. This is something that I consider slightly more shameless than commend-
able. It is an unblushing confession of guilt, but the guilt is still
there.

There are times when the guilt is deliberate, when it is pur-
poseful and not guilt at all, but the author is still doubtful
whether the audience will know what he is doing. Here, again,

he will make an attempt to cover himself. An example of this occurred in *I Am a Camera*. In the last act of that play, after the appearance of her mother, Sally Bowles, the heroine, disappeared for a long while as a character of any dominance. She had controlled almost every scene so far, and I received complaints during the out-of-town tryout that she seemed suddenly to have left the cast. This was intentional on my part, but I did not relish the thought that it looked like a dramatic mistake. Here, then, I inserted a "cover line," somewhat as Barrie had done, but not with the intention of admitting that I knew I was making an error. The hero, seeing what was happening to Sally and her envelopment by her mother, cries out: "Sally, don't let her. You're disappearing in front of my eyes." This line was a belated insertion, but it still seems to me a good and wise one. It seemed to me to remove a blame for something which I was doing quite deliberately.

It was seldom that Barrie made that kind of mistake. He could normally handle technical problems superbly. In *Dear Brutus* he was up against a serious one. The first act of that play is set in a country house. There are windows across the back, showing a garden. It is essential to the act that the backdrop must be changed while it is in progress, and the garden be removed for a magically substituted wood. The curtains must, therefore, be open when the act starts, be closed during it, and then opened again—and with a quality of surprise—at the end. How to get them closed? Easy. A woman character can say that she is cold, that there is a draft from the open window, and request the closing of it, and of the curtains. Easy, perhaps, but almost certainly fatal. That same ugly fellow in the gallery would notice it, would wonder why that line of dialogue had been inserted, and at the end, when the curtains were opened again, there would be no surprise, only a murmur of "So that was what it was for." What does Barrie do? His philanderer character is making love to another woman in the room. His wife passes on the terrace outside. She sees what is happening, and enters:

> I am sorry to interrupt you, Jack, but please wait a moment before you kiss her again. Excuse me, Joanna.
> *(She closes the curtains)*
> I did not want the others to see you. They might not understand how noble you are, Jack. You can go on now.
> *(She exits by the door)*

The trick has been pulled. The wife's line has got a laugh, we know her relationship with her husband, and the curtains have been closed without anyone's noticing the fact. The surprise at the end will work now.

Everything should, if possible, be made to serve two purposes like this. The conjurer with his legerdemain knows that fact, and is perfectly prepared for his sleight of hand to be noticed, provided the audience thinks he is using it for the wrong purpose. The dramatist should know it, too. Ibsen knew it. In *The Wild Duck*, the mess that Gregers Werle makes, determined to do everything for himself, when he lights his own fire and then tries to put it out with a water jug, this detail serves two purposes. It is symbolic of the way that Gregers handles his whole life and everyone else's, and it also makes it essential for an important interview which would normally take place in his own room to happen on the stage. This is good technique, and it also takes a lot of careful thought and skill in writing.

The same kind of device must be employed whenever a prop is to be used. This is especially so with guns and weapons of death. These do not normally occur in ordinary houses, and the audience's attention must be called to them, but never in such a way that it realizes, instantly, what is being done and that the instrument is to be later employed for its own purpose. The best of all ways is to introduce it with a laugh, but that is not easy with guns. Nor of Indian krises, nor South American blowpipes laden with a deadly and undecipherable poison. I do not know how those are to be introduced, but if you are going to employ them, you have got to manage it, and unnoticeably. It is wiser to avoid them, unless you are writing out-and-out melodrama, and even there they need some apparently innocent coverage.

Do not, similarly, resort to the telephone's being out of order, the delayed telegram, the letter with insufficient stamps, so that you can get your characters where and when they would not normally be. I know that telephones do go out of order—you can get a playful child, God forbid, to put it out of order—and that telegrams get infuriatingly delayed in real life, but a play is not real life. This fact must never be forgotten. It is real life presented selectively and with a purpose; that ugly fellow in the gallery knows all about that; it is your job, as playwright, to make him forget it. The man who can shout from the gallery is your most invaluable critic. Do not have characters receive letters, and then discover that they have left their glasses upstairs so that someone else has to read the letter to them. Do not have them leave the stage because the milk in the kitchen must be boiling over. Again, milk does boil over, but that particular milk boiling over at that particular time is too obvious a convenience. I could list a hundred more like this.

But, the playwright will exclaim in despair, how am I to do it? I must have that letter read aloud, I must get Aunt Jane off the stage, I must have the heroine arrive unexpectedly. Those ways are the only ways by which I can achieve those things. That, actually, is never true. Dodie Smith once invented a first maxim for playwrights: "There is no technical problem that cannot be solved." She meant by this that anything can be done, that there is always a better way, and that there is no such word for the dramatist as "can't." It may take hours and hours to think out that better way, it may need going right back to your first act and planting some preparation there, and that preparation may well lead on to other things as well. It should do so. If it is essential that the telephone is out of order, if your plot will not work unless it is out of order, then you had better have an off-stage windstorm to put it out of order. Having invented the windstorm, you will have to make it cover other things, produce other results, and these results will probably shape your story a little differently. When the time arrives for your telephone to be out of order, it will seem like a normal incident in your fabric. Playwriting, apart from being like a lot of other things, is also very like chess, where a whole series of moves must be made to lead up to the one you want. Each of these moves will lead to other moves. And the ultimate aim of none of them should be apparent. Never let your telephone be just plainly and simply out of order.

There was a prejudice when I was young against using the telephone in plays, because it was a comparatively new invention. Nowadays it is a part of everyday life, and it is used as such in the theater. It can, of course, be over-used. Just as one grows irritated with the friends in real life who come into one's house and then settle down to telephone or be telephoned to, so are authors in the same position. Telephone if you must, but remember that there are other people in the room wanting to talk to you. Telephone scenes are very popular with actors. They give them the chance for a pure piece of solo acting, with no one else to endanger the tempo, and they look as if they were being played with another actor whom the telephoner can characterize at will. If the author has written them well, they can often get the actor a hand at the end of them. There is no reason why a playwright should be too highly bred to remember this.

The radio and the television set are newer intrusions into real life. They have not yet been proved very valuable in the theater, being connected with an impersonal world. The radio is an irritation on the stage. It is either pure addition to the play, an attempt to dress it up most illegitmately (I had a whole record made of a radio sketch, supposed to have been acted by Olive in *The Voice of the Turtle,* and I cut it out after one performance), or else it is used to disperse vital news at the right moment, when it smacks too strongly of necessity. So far, I have seen television used only briefly in *Point of No Return* and *Remains To Be Seen.* It will probably be essayed, as motion pictures have been used in the theater, and I doubt if it will be any more successful, or longer surviving.

There are other things which are attractive to try to do, and which are seldom successful either. Parties are very hard to handle on stage. With our present kind of theater, I would say that large parties are impossible. The audience cannot listen to more than one set of speakers at the same time. The device of having the others mouth in silence while Mr. A. and Mrs. B. are talking is no longer excusable. The audience will either see that the actors are saying nothing at all, or will try to do some lip-reading to see what they are whispering, and the proper conversation goes unheard. Never let actors sit and whisper "Rhu-barb" at each other. (I do not know why "Rhubarb," but that is what they are normally supposed to murmur at such times.) Never have two conversations going on at once, and never try to pretend that what is said at one side of the stage cannot be heard at the other side. The audience will not go with you in this fiction. If you need a large party for your play, then you must have it happening in the next room, with doors that can be closed when you want private conversation. The room on stage will be an adjunct to the party, a place to which the guests can overflow. Once a door is closed, anything can be said. All doors are soundproof in the theater. Remember this, and the fact that speeches made off stage, as well as speeches made in the dark, are almost certain to be inaudible to the audience. It is not a bad idea to give characters certain lines to speak as they leave, and even in the outside hall, but never make them of any value or importance beyond that of mere atmosphere.

The outside hall suggests another question. To what extent has the rest of a stage house any value? The outside hall, partly visible, and the invisible front door in *I Am a Camera* have con-siderable value, I think, in creating more of that rooming apart-ment, especially as the room shown has only one door. The orchestra playing below stage in the dance scene of *The Damask Cheek* helped to create the downstairs of that house. Again, a single detail can help more than a dozen could. When I started that play I grew worried over the bedroom space that the house should contain, especially as it was a New York house of a pe-riod with which I was unfamiliar. My collaborator, Lloyd Mor-ris, obligingly drew me a complete set of plans of the house, detailed down to the closets. This was of use in helping the house to become a real one for me, but I doubt, now, if it served any other valuable purpose. The author should know his house, and then forget it largely while writing. Yet the house must exist. The audience should be able to visualize the actor going somewhere when he leaves the stage, and not just into the wings. The off-stage rooms must have reality for the audience, but it cannot be swamped in their details. Let me say again that it is the selection of detail that is most important in plays. Too much and the audience is bored, too little and it will not have absorbed what it should.

Novelists, it was once thought, had weather all to themselves, and it was believed that there was no weather in the theater, outside of the howling (and never very believable) winds in *King Lear* and the paper snowstorm into which the melodramatic father used to turn his daughter. This is not true, however. Weather, off-stage weather especially, can contribute a great deal to a play, especially to the more modern play of mood. It is hard to portray physically on stage—though stage rain can be managed—but the right lines, again a very few of them, can do a great deal to create it. I have always felt that the five lines creating the spring in the last scene of *The Voice of the Turtle* had a great deal of value. So, for me, had the off-stage blizzard which the heroine watches through the window and speaks of when her heart is breaking, in *Old Acquaintance*. Carson McCullers uses weather exquisitely in the last scene of *The Member of the Wedding* when Berenice speaks of the past and tragic month.

The most beautiful September I ever seen. Countless white and yellow butterflies flying around them autumn flowers—Honey dead and John Henry suffering like he did—and daisies, golden weather, butterflies—such strange death weather.

Four lines, and a picture has been created. Rain, wind, mist, drizzle, sunlight and moonlight can all be brought into the theater by the author who has felt and seen them. Remember the moon that "tips with silver all these fruit-tree tops" in *Romeo and Juliet*. Scene-painting would be weak against the illusion that is created there. We are in the garden with the lovers. In those days, there were no scenic designers, and it is well for the playwright if he can pretend to himself that there still are none, and that he has to paint his picture for himself. It will repay him.

It is really the scene designer who has hurt the outdoor set in the theater. I have never cared for exterior scenes, and have avoided them where possible. This is due mainly to modern stage mechanics, to the look of stage grass which is never like real grass, any more than stage flowers ever look like real flowers, and to the creases in the sky. And also, for this very reason, to the fact that the more real they look, the more the audience is inclined to whisper over them. Remember that audiences are very like a group of children, and get an absurd pleasure out of seeing something that really works. This can damage the attention that they give to the play. It has reminded them that they are in a theater, which is what the playwright set himself out to avoid. Equally, however, they can become annoyed when things do not work as they should, and they can start to whisper over that, too. That is why the taps in *The Voice of the Turtle* really ran water. Audiences used to whisper over them, and I knew that the play had momentarily gone out of the window. But I knew, too, that it would have gone out to a greater extent if the taps had not worked at all.

Those taps caused me a lot of trouble. They were treated by some critics as though they were a part of the play, and had been designed to contribute to its success. They even seemed to diminish the play slightly. I knew there was both value and danger in letting the audience play house, but once I had decided to set the play in a whole apartment, showing three rooms, I was forced to have things that worked. The trouble was, mainly, that several of them were new things that audiences were not accustomed to seeing in the theater; the taps, for instance. If scene-designing had reached a point where real grass, real flowers, a truthful sky-looking sky could be put on stage, the first few plays that employed them would suffer in just that way. After that, the audience would be used to them. At the present moment, no exterior has managed to look very like a real exterior, and that is why I have chosen to avoid them, preferring to bring my characters indoors from the open air, and then to re-create the outside world in dialogue, though never in set speeches whose only purpose was quite obviously just to do that. The references have to be slid in, jostling against something else, backed by another purpose in the same speech. If you have a character look out of the window and describe what he sees in the way of nature with no reason other than a scenic description, the audience will know what you are doing, and will reel away from it as the average reader will retreat from a passage of pure description in a fast-moving novel.

All of this will apply to other things than weather. Your audience is anxious to share in all your characters' tastes, if you can bring them alive to it, even down to the taste for food, of a longed-for cigarette (the audience longs for it, too, and the actors' cigarettes taste better than its own would do), or a steak served to a hungry man. There was a poorish play in London which I attended once without having had any dinner beforehand. In the second act, the characters had champagne and caviar sandwiches, and the lack of the play's appeal was sufficient to send me out after the act to chase up the same things for myself. Had the play's appeal been stronger, I should have participated in the character's pleasure and forgotten my own. The skillful author will never forget this. It applies to everything in mood-writing, to every detail carefully selected that can make the mood more real and more vivid to the audience. The off-stage chiming of the stable clock in the reflective nursery scene in *Dear Octopus* is an example of this, and the character who remarks on all the associations he has with that chime is expressing the sensations of the audience deeply imbedded with his own.

There is nothing that cannot add to the mood if it is conceived rightly. There is a further example from *I Am a Camera*, which has an interesting side-light to it. This concerns the brief description of the funeral of an ex-liberal leader which is filling the streets of Berlin on that day in 1930. It is mentioned, slightly described, slightly discussed. It has nothing to do with the plot of the play at all. When we were engaged on cutting the play, which was a good deal overlength at its tryout, it was suggested to me that I cut this funeral out entirely. It proved nothing, I was told. I was all ready to cut it, but one of my producers objected violently. He insisted that it made a vivid living picture of Berlin in those days, that it created streets, people, mood, and that it was as valuable as any piece of scenery could be. I left the speeches in, and have since seen him proved right by a critic who commented on the funeral as a vital section of the off-stage life of that period, contributing most valuably to the play.

Again, it is selectiveness that counts. What do you decide to include, what to omit? You can have a hundred details in your head, and they can all of them be good ones. You must select two, at the outside, two, and make them do the work of the rest. Remember the cherry orchard in the play of that name, and the love with which Chekhov painted it. Remember the memory that Madame Ranevsky has of herself as a child, waking to see the trees all white, and her vision of her mother, dressed in white, moving down the long avenue. Remember the care with which these have been picked, and how they linger in your memory and seem to suggest other details which you will not find in the play. Stage writing is like the decoration of a well-proportioned room. Once, you could have cozy corners, and pile ornaments and objects on every shelf. Nowadays, you select the few, the representative few. They will do the work for you, and you can see the room as well. That is how you should detail your plays.

Lastly, there is that thing called the "*scène à faire.*" This means the obligatory scene, the scene that the playwright is forced to write by the exigencies of his plot. The books on craftsmanship are full of it. Archer has a dozen examples. You take a play about a young man who has an unknown illegitimate brother or sister. (So many plays used to be all about that; were there more of those in the older days?) The "*scène à faire*" is the scene where they discover the fact, and of their meeting as such. This is understandable. We have all recognized such scenes coming way ahead of themselves. In *A Streetcar Named Desire* the scene of the rape was an obligatory scene. We foresaw it, we knew it had to happen, it would have been a serious mistake to have left it off stage. The last line of that scene indicates its necessity to us: "We've had this date with each other from the beginning." The audience had had the date, too, and it had to be fulfilled. The disillusionment scene with Mitch in the same play is equally obligatory. There was a story that used to be told in conferences in motion picture studios. If you have planted a volcano early in the picture, and have planted the danger of its eruption, you cannot finish the picture without showing that eruption. You cannot have a character remark: "You remember that volcano that we were all afraid would erupt? Well, it erupted last night." The eruption was the "*scène à faire*." You had to write it.

But there are "*scènes à faire*" that we dread having to watch, knowing that they must come upon us. This is more likely to happen when they are many than when they are few. There are those plays in which a number of people are facing a joint disaster which they will have to meet separately, a trial or a decision which each must encounter on his own. How well we all know the moment when we glance at our programs, and realize that there are still five more to go. This must surely have happened in *The Passing of the Third Floor Back*. The author will be cheered who can devise a satisfactory means of cutting down on them. If even one character had quietly died offstage, there would have been thanks murmured in the audience.

It is perhaps partly for this reason, as well as for others, that playwrights have often found it is better to avoid what looked like an obligatory scene, and to play it off stage. This is done, too, where the audience knows exactly what the content of the scene is to be. Priestley was faced with this in *Eden End*, where the daughter has to tell her father that she is married to the cheap actor. The audience knows that fact, and it knows all its details; the construction has set it that way. It does not want to hear them all again, merely to witness the father's distress. Priestley has ended his second act with the girl going to her father's room, saying: "You can't begin to understand how hateful this is going to be for me." He raises the curtain on his third act, after the scene is over. A French playwright of the sixties would have frowned on this, but it seems to me a wise thing.

In the same way, never if possible (and everything is always possible) tell the audience a story twice, make it listen to the same things twice over, because another character has to be told them. How well Ibsen realized this in *The Wild Duck*, when he made Gregers take Hjalmar for a long walk to tell him the truth about his marriage and his life. It would seem here again that this was a "*scène à faire*," since it is the burden of the plot, but by handling it this way, Ibsen managed to avoid making it a "*scène à faire deux fois*." Hjalmar's succeeding scene when he returns to his home is the better for our not having heard just what has been said to him.

There is another evasion of what looks like an obligatory scene in G. K. Chesterton's *Magic*, where the conjurer gives a false explanation of how his miracle was performed to the boy who is having a nervous breakdown because he cannot believe in supernatural interference. The scene is played off stage, and very speedily, almost too speedily. The evasion of it is justified when the conjurer returns, and explains what he has done. He is asked what he told the boy. He refuses to tell, saying that the trick had been worked by magic, but that if he repeated the lie to them, they would all believe it as the boy had done. The only objection to this is that the boy will recover, and will repeat the explanation himself. But that is beyond the purlieus of the play, and I should probably not have thought of it. You may perhaps tell me that the real reason for omitting the scene was that the author could not, himself, think up a convincing lie. In that case, I can only say that he managed to cover himself admirably.

Quite often, too, it is the preparation rather than the scene itself that is effective. Anyone who has seen *Grand Guignol* plays will have realized that it is the mounting of the expected horror that produces the grisliness of the evening. The detail and the preparation of the scene, the characters happy and innocent at first, then growing slowly aware of the doom that may descend on them—these are the things, far more than the actual putting out of the eyes, that produce nausea in the audience. We have read reviews, we have seen other *Grand Guignol* plays, we can picture the beastliness of the moment, but it is the slow preparation of the instruments that sickens us. The moment of horror is really the release, even though it is always actually shown; but that is the purpose of that kind of play.

In *The Member of the Wedding*, Carson McCullers laid herself open to similar charges of omission. The purpose of her play to some extent absolves her from blame, though not, I think, altogether. Almost all the real action of the play happens off stage between Scenes 1 and 2 of the third act. I know that in the original version, as played at the tryout, there was a scene between Frankie and the soldier, a scene that was in the novel from which the play was adapted. This scene, the whole incident, though actually not all the preparation for it, has been removed, but there still seems to be a good deal taking place outside our view. And there is one scene omitted earlier that seems to me a vital "*scène à faire*." Frankie has determined that she is going with her brother and his new wife on their wedding trip. That is the basic interest of the play. She has to make the proposal to them. We know that they will refuse it, and we know, too, that their refusal will break her heart. But this scene is played off stage. It is a brokenhearted Frankie who runs back on, and I feel that we should have seen her heart broken. I know that I felt cheated here, and began to mutter to myself, like any old professor, about the obligatory scene.

For the most part, however, I appreciated very well what Carson McCullers was doing in this play and what she was after. Her plot was of small importance to her. The only trouble was that there was a sudden rush of it, off stage. She was aiming at an inside study of loneliness, and adolescence, and the hazards of fate and mischance. She achieved something, too, which had long been in my own mind as something that I wanted to see done—probably to do myself—in the theater, and that was the use of a sudden, senseless and dramatically unprepared death, such as happens in real life when a person can walk out of a room perfectly happily, and be killed in an automobile accident ten minutes later. The best example I have ever known of this in fiction occurs with the death of Mrs. Proudie in *The Last Chronicle of Barset*, when the other characters and the reader are eagerly awaiting her appearance at a conference at which she will make herself typically and entertainingly unpleasant. Then the maid arrives and begs her master to come quickly to her mistress. Mrs. Proudie has died of a heart attack in her room. I have read that the reason for this incident was that Trollope was in his club one day and overheard another member declaring that he was sick to death of Mrs. Proudie as a character. Trollope went home, and killed her that afternoon. Carson McCullers lets her child, John Henry, die of meningitis just as swiftly and unexpectedly, though for a better reason. When the news came that he was ill, there was a sudden tiny shudder through the theater, and I felt that I had seen a master's touch in action.

I have given a great deal of time to this play. I have asked myself why. It had many faults, a shadowiness in its lesser characters amounting almost to non-existence of some of them, a faulty construction, and several others. It is not a play for beginners to follow unless they are aware of these. But I think it was the last new play that I have seen that deeply impressed me. I saw it three times, as I saw *The Glass Menagerie* three times, and I have read it several times as well. I have tried to see how it achieved the things that made it so moving and so novel. Each time the method has escaped me. I can attribute this only to its total honesty, and to the author's absorption in what she was doing. She wrote nothing that was not of the deepest truth and significance to her, and she was completely immersed in her mood. For all the play's faults, the mood remains wholly pervasive. Together with *The Glass Menagerie,* and other forerunners, it may have helped to open that door into a newer kind of theater. If so, I shall be the first to cheer and to try to follow the way through it.

CHAPTER THIRTEEN

The Closing of the Acts

ANYONE, it has been said, can write a good first act. This remark, it seems to me, is based on a half-conception of what a first act must contain. It is considered easy because the characters are new and fresh, the situations are being prepared, and there are apparently few constructional problems to be dealt with. It is all introduction. But a first act must also have movement, it cannot seem like all preparation, it must interest the audience, prepare it for what is going to happen, and yet seem to have a life of its own. I have never found a first act easy to write. I have indicated before my own slowness, my sense that the ground must be turned over and over again, and also a certain fear—based largely on my awareness of my weakness with plot—that I will not have enough incident to go around if I start too soon. Long ago, when Auriol Lee was directing my plays, she and I were in the habit of saying to each other: "If the audience will come back after the first act, we shall be all right."

A too good and too full first act can do harm. The other acts will seem to lessen in power and interest. You cannot always tell in advance. I had been under the impression, at every rehearsal, that the first act of *I Am a Camera* was the least good of the play. When it was performed, and audience laughter and attention could be measured, it turned out just the other way around. On the other hand, I had no idea until I saw it played, that the first act of *The Druid Circle* was as flat and unmoving as it proved to be, or that the second would play as well as it did. These are things that only performance can teach you, and usually they teach it to you too late to be of any help with that especial play. Your key and your tempo have been set, and it is almost impossible to speed or ginger up a dull first act. Its dullness or otherwise was set for you when you first conceived what it would contain, at what point in your characters' lives you would raise your curtain.

There have been many rules about first acts. Too many of these rules are apt to stick in our heads. It is a bad thing how casual remarks can stay in a young practitioner's mind. When I was very young I read in a book of play reviews that the first act of a certain play was merely introductory, "as almost all first acts are." I cannot remember now where this phrase occurred. Its authorship matters only because the remark itself has haunted me all of my playwriting lifetime, and always to my disadvantage, and I would like to do anything I can to cancel it out. There are books that children and young people should not read. Their phrases lie over into grown-up life. First acts are not merely introductory, or if they are, they should not be. I will continue to beg myself to obliterate that memory, as I will all other playwrights. They must introduce everything, I know, but their purpose must go further than that; they must not merely introduce, they must get things started. And they must show the way that the play is going.

I am loath, after what I have just said about the too-long-remembered remarks, to add another to them, but there is one piece of real advice that has been personally handed to me that I am eager to pass on. It came from Arnold Bennett, that most distinguished of novelists, who was not a bad hand at play-writing, himself. *Milestones* is still a fine play; read it some-time. It was after seeing the tryout of a play of mine that he told me that at the end of my first act he still had no idea of where I was going, and that that was a very serious fault. The first-act curtain, he assured me, must be a signpost to the au-dience of where it is being taken. The author's purpose, the main issue of the play, must be indicated there. This is some-thing I have never forgotten.

Let us for a moment examine a few plays, taken more or less at random, and see this illustrated. The first act of *Mrs. Tan-queray* ends after Paula's brief threat of committing suicide if anything bad ever happens to her again, with her exit on the words: "I'm so happy." Nothing, I think, could be clearer than that. The first act of *Candida* ends with the young poet proclaim-ing he is the happiest of mortals, and the clergyman husband saying: "So was I—an hour ago." The first-act curtain of *Re-union in Vienna* is when the heroine, Elena, who has two min-utes earlier denied any beauty to the old Viennese waltz tunes, is left alone with her father-in-law, suddenly retracts her judgment, agrees that the "Dollar Princess Waltz" is beautiful, holds out her arms and dances with him. This is the needed sign that homesickness for the old days still has power over her, and that she is going to the party that night. All of these indicate exactly what Arnold Bennett was after—the signpost to the audience.

The first act of *Night Must Fall* ends with Danny unconsciously singing "Mighty Lak a Rose" as he works, the song that betrays him as the looked-for murderer. And the first act of *The Member of the Wedding* ends with the heroine's exact statement of the play's theme: "I love the two of them so much, and we belong to be together. I love the two of them so much, because they are the *we* of me." Of these examples, it is significant that they all end with a piece of wholly revealing business, or a line that could almost be a soliloquy—the character's own statement, whether conscious or unconscious, of what the thesis of the play is. In less skillful hands, we get the kind of line that the author speaks for them, also often near to a soliloquy: "That's what *you* think," or "I wonder." That is telling the audience with a vengeance, but the author has at least recognized the need to do so.

The second-act curtain, in a three-act play, is the big curtain, where the biggest punch is thrown, and the only pulling of that punch should be a deliberate one, to make it more effective. This is where the play must show the hold that it has taken. The second act is the piling up of all the forces, the raising of the plot to its highest and most suspenseful strength. It is the meat and the guts of the play, and the curtain should emphasize that fact. It is foolish to be above or afraid of the effective curtain, and to speak of it derisively as a "click" curtain. Once, the fashion was for picture curtains—the heroine fainting in her lover's arms, or the hero all trussed up and ready to be dynamited. From these it moved on to the effective line curtain, and a writer as skillful and as modern as S. N. Behrman has not shied away from that usage. The second-act curtain of *Rain from Heaven* is where the heroine, whose visitors are attacking her Jewish refugee friend, steps in to say: "Hobart, please remember—Herr Willens is not only my lover, he is also my guest." That could have come from any drama of the eighteen-nineties, except that in that case the word "lover" would have been a deliberate lie to protect the Jew. Perhaps, too, the line might have been reversed, and the word "lover" put last. Today a reminder of civility under such circumstances has more dramatic power.

The click curtain line, hitting the situation right on the nose, is wonderful when it occurs to you. It is probably the best second-act curtain that can be written. Let us take a few more examples. The second-act curtain of *Life with Father* is Mr. Day's sudden realization of what he has let himself in for—his promise to be baptized, which has been the turning point of the plot. It also leads on beautifully to the last act. The second act of *Born Yesterday* ends with the newly rebellious heroine's line to her protector: "Would you do me a favor, Harry? Drop dead!" Act Two of *The Voice of the Turtle* ends with the turning out of the bedroom light, and the heroine's desperate cry of "We must keep this gay!" This curtain—the sex inference of it—I knew in advance. I was not quite clear as to how I would get to it until I arrived at it on paper. In the printed version, there is an extra line of dialogue that I hoped would be heard, but the laugh on Sally's line never failed to drown it, and we let it go in performance. *The Corn Is Green* ends its second act with the opening of the examination papers (again what the play is most keenly about), and the schoolmistress' thankful murmur, as she looks at them, of "Henry the Eighth," the subject she had prompted the boy to reread. Act Two of *The Silver Cord* ends with Mrs. Phelps trying to stop her sons from going to the rescue of the girl she has driven to attempt suicide, calling after them through the window: "Robin, you're not dressed! Dave, get your coat! Are you crazy? Do you *want* to catch pneumonia?" And Act Two of *Arsenic and Old Lace* ends with the timely and gay entrance of the unconscious victim who will overbalance the at present equal murder account. Your second-act curtain is usually a vigorous underlining of what you have spent your evening in trying to do.

The opposite kind of click curtain, the click curtain taken in reverse, the punch deliberately pulled, is again best exemplified in *The Member of the Wedding*. It is actually only a scene curtain, but it is one of the most moving I have ever seen staged. Tragedy has broken loose in the household, and Berenice, the colored cook, is sitting trembling at the thought of what may be happening off stage at that moment. With her is the small child, John Henry. The lights have gone out in a thunderstorm, and the stage is lit by a candle only.

JOHN HENRY

I'm scared. Where's Honey?

BERENICE

Jesus knows. I'm scared, too. With Honey snow-crazy, and loose like this—and Frankie run off with her Papa's pistol. I feel like every nerve has been picked out of me.

JOHN HENRY

(Holding out his sea-shell, and stroking Berenice)

You want to listen to the ocean?

There is magic in that curtain, the magic of another world and of sounds beyond this life. It is like a Chekhov curtain, one of the finest of which is based on the minor tragedy of anticlimax. In the third act of *Uncle Vanya*, the girl and her stepmother, after a long period of animosity, have come together in a most touching scene. They are happy at last. They long for music. The stepmother tells the girl to go and and ask her father, who is still awake, whether he will mind if she plays. The girl goes off stage. Yelena has a tiny soliloquy. "It's a long time since I have played the piano. I shall play, and cry, cry like an idiot." Sonia returns. She has one line. "We mustn't." The curtain descends. The audience will, I think, be suddenly in tears.

It was the memory of curtains such as these that led me to devise in rehearsal the second-act curtain of *I Am a Camera*. I wanted the same sense of anticlimax topping a scene of happiness, but a more chilling one, a sudden splitting of two viewpoints. Chris and Sally have had a gay and absurd scene together, following on a disappointment. Suddenly he gets the idea that they are still miles apart, that she has changed in nothing, has learned nothing from their recent lesson, while he, himself, has. Sally sees his disapproving face; she tries to force him back to laughter; she laughs herself to coax him on. He tries to join her, but his laughter fails. Then hers fails, too, and they move slowly apart from each other. This, as I say, was created at rehearsal, and it needs the perfect timing of movement, the exact beat of laughter rising and then failing to complete its rise, the split second when the curtain must fall on their move away from each other to achieve its exact purpose. But when the timing had been accomplished, it achieved what I wanted—a sudden and chilling split between two people. The earlier curtain that I had written omitted the split, and played only on Sally's ridiculous and unconscious personal vanity. It led me nowhere.

The third and last curtain is a rounding out of the entertainment. It has many forms. The last act, in any case, is the most difficult of them all. No one, I think, doubts that. Too many plays have been ruined by bad last acts. That is why one can still wonder sometimes whether it should not be written or, at any rate, constructed first, to be sure that it has a valid existence, as the last act of Cinderella has. Yet to construct it that well, that far in advance, would destroy for me the sense of free invention, the sense that the play was carrying me along with it. One must be sure, however, that there *is* a last act, that the play has somewhere to go, to develop to, and that it will not end in a dead rut. Then, being sure of that, I will take my chance. I am not recommending this as good advice. It has not always saved me. I have found myself in dead ruts; I have sometimes got out of them, and sometimes I have not. In more cases than one when so situated, I have gone back and reread my first two acts very carefully, and I have found a detail, a line of dialogue which, while I had no idea when I wrote it of what purpose it could serve, has given me a possible—I will not call it more—last act to develop from it.

Last acts, if the plot has not a clear-cut and straight-line ending of its own, very often need devices to keep them going, and to help them over bad patches. New characters can do this— they have done it for me in *Young Woodley* and in *The Distaff Side*—enlivening the audience with a new interest when it is most needed. These must, of course, be characters who are well prepared for, and for whom the audience's curiosity has been whetted. Their appearance will satisfy a need to see them. This awareness of an audience's need and the satisfying of it are essentials to a dramatist. The audience cannot be deprived of that satisfaction. I spoke earlier of the question of revenge and of paying out the villain. This is a deep need. It has filled many last acts. When it is essential that the villain shall be murdered, that being the only way to remove him from the cast and satisfy the audience by leaving the hero and heroine free at last, the question of who is to perform the murder is a troublesome one. Everyone in the audience wants to see him murdered, but no sympathetic member of the cast can perform it. That is why I always suspect the presence of the half-wit or idiot native in a list of characters. It is almost always he who will do the deed, and then can be excused for his half-wittedness. After it, he can slink back to the jungle or the local asylum, and the hero and heroine can go off together.

This need for revenge does not always have to be satisfied by murder, but the villain cannot be allowed to go scot-free. If the heroine has been made to suffer, the audience wants to see her not only righted, but also avenged. The villain must suffer, too. There is a most excellent example of this in *His House in Order*, a play with a most excellent plot, in which the author, realizing the double need of the audience, was determined to give it the best of both worlds. Nina in that play has been humiliated by her in-laws, compared always to her discredit with her predecessor, the dead first wife. At last, she has the power to revenge herself, to prove the dead wife worthless and to humiliate the family. She wants to do so. Everyone in the audience would like to see her do so, but they know, too, that she must not, that she will lose her sympathy and her appeal for them if she reveals the contents of the incriminating letters to the wrong people. Nina is talked out of it. She becomes a true heroine when she releases the letters to her sympathetic brother-in-law to destroy, or to do what he likes with. She lets herself be trodden further underfoot. One-half of the job is done here. The heroine has had her wish for revenge and has sacrificed it. She has behaved well. The other half has now to be dealt with. In the last act, when the in-laws have gotten even worse, the brother-in-law, the man who talked her out of her revenge, takes matters into his own hands, and gives the letters to her husband. The in-laws are expelled, and a happy ending would seem likely. Everyone is satisfied.

This awareness that the heroine will be lowered in the audience's esteem if she takes the revenge that the audience longs to see taken is an odd thing. It is a quirk in human nature, and I do not approve of it, even though I share it. I would like to see one-half of it stamped out, and have either the revenge or its renunciation eliminated, instead of playing it both ways and having someone else manage it. As it stands, it seems to me that both the worthy and the unworthy sides of human nature are being satisfied, and that feels a little like hypocrisy. But the audience being composed of human beings, that side of their nature has to be taken into account and gratified.

It takes a man of keen sense to be aware of this situation in all its gradations. The first time that I saw *The Barretts of Wimpole Street* I felt, when the curtain rose on the last scene, that the author had made a mistake. The interest, it seemed to me, lay with the young lovers, and now that they had departed, there was no more play. I could not have been more seriously wrong. When Mr. Barrett opens the letters and decides on revenging himself weakly, uselessly, on Elizabeth's dog, the sister, Henrietta, announces that Elizabeth has taken the dog away with her. This is the ending to the play. It would never have occurred to me that it was as essential as it was shown to be when the audience burst into delighted applause on the line, without waiting for the curtain. I had not recognized that it was necessary to the audience to see Mr. Barrett kicked in the face, but Rudolph Besier, the playwright, knew it. He knew, too, that Elizabeth could not deliver the kick. It must happen through her, and yet despite her. Henrietta takes it from her in that line, because it is an unsuitable scene for the heroine to play, but the scene has to be played, and the play is not finished until it has been.

That, too, is part of the secret of the last-act curtain, that awareness of what the audience has yet to see, what it needs still to see. The decision for this is all the author's. I would not have had Rudolph Besier's awareness over Mr. Barrett. A great many people (of whom I am most definitely not one) have never agreed with Bernard Shaw in *Saint Joan*. To them, the play ends after the burning of Joan, and the epilogue is a piece of unnecessary afterthought. To me, the epilogue is essential if the play is to have any meaning at all. The scene before it (the scene which ends what the dissenters call the play) closes with the line that I have quoted above, the line of: "I wonder." I have never cared for this. To me it would end better with the executioner's line that precedes it: "You have heard the last of her," and then let the epilogue do all the wondering, but my guess would be that Shaw inserted the line, aware perhaps of its weakness, to indicate that there was more to come. The last line of the epilogue states the whole play and its message: "O

God that madest this beautiful earth, when will it be ready to receive Thy saints? How long, O Lord, how long?" I know of few better endings than this one.

The last line of the play must complete the emotion, underline it for us, mark its closing. The older-fashioned picture curtain of the lovers embracing is still in favor here, because if the play is a romantic one, the audience will wait for it. Otherwise, the moment that the end is in sight, the moment the situation is relaxed, there is a speedy movement beneath the seats for hats, and the last few minutes disappear. That is why so many authors try to hold the interest and the suspense until the last second, and then drop the curtain the moment they are discharged. It is safer to do it that way, especially in melodrama, but it can also seem sudden and perfunctory. No story ever ends, except with death, with full completeness; there is always more that can and will happen to the characters that one feels the author should at least indicate. Even suicides can seem a conveniently abrupt finish. (I might perhaps add here that authors should be sparing of suicides. You can only handle a few in your dramatic lifetime, and you had better save them until they are absolutely essential to you.) To me, even the death of a leading character needs a resolution and comment, too. It can be as good as the one in *Hamlet,* or as bad as the one in *Romeo and Juliet,* but in neither play was the curtain rung down on their deaths. Hedda Gabler's suicide has an almost unbearably ironic epitaph spoken over it, and so has the Master Builder's tragic end.

The last curtain of *A Doll's House* is—or was—a classic. The slamming of that door echoed for the next fifty years in the theater. Today perhaps it seems a little like a trick. But all curtains are tricks. It is a trick to shut out a view of life at the most appropriate moment. The whole of stage technique is a trick, and the author's job is to use it as skillfully as he can, and either to conceal its trickiness or else to reveal it quite deliberately. There is another trick for a last-act curtain which makes no bones about being merely a device. This is the repeat of the first-act curtain, sometimes of a whole first-act scene, to mark a sense of repetition in a play and so achieve an ending. It was used in *The Green Bay Tree, The Wind and the Rain, White Cargo* and also in *Jane Clegg,* in which play the curtain of each act is the same, the extinction of the lights and the family going to bed. The device is a little familiar by now, and the playwright will avoid it if he can, but it can still work satisfactorily if adroitly handled. The audience can almost be induced to speak the last line for you.

I have, myself, a weakness for another kind of ending to a play, a slowly dying end, comparable to the fading of colors into a twilight. I think a certain amount of this partiality has been due to my early admiration for the ending of *The Madras House,* where the last dialogue for husband and wife dwindles into an affectionate silence, with the stage direction: "She does not finish, for really there is no end to the subject. But for a moment or two longer, happy together, they stand looking into the fire." I know that average audiences are not with me in this. It is equivalent to making the last scene almost an epilogue. I did it in *The Distaff Side,* where the story of the play was over once the young heroine had chosen her man, which was at the end of the first scene of the last act. But I, myself, had not finished. I still had things to say, things that I wanted to portray. I anticipated the hat-reaching by staging a row with the grandmother, taking down the first curtain while it was at its noisiest height, and I wrote the last scene as a gentle epilogue on the early morning of the heroine's departure for America. I did the same thing, after the heroine's death at the end of Act Three, Scene 1, in a play called *Gertie Maude*. In both cases, I was more than satisfied with what I had done, though both have been adversely commented on. To me, it was as though the forces, now expended, were being gathered together like embers for their own last gentle warmth, and the curtain stole down to hide the people. When that method succeeds, there is a very gentle sigh of satisfaction in the audience that is a deeply welcome sound in the theater. It is a little like the dismissal with praise of a good servant after a long evening's work.

CHAPTER FOURTEEN

The New Play

I HAVE finished. I have passed on all I know. And it seems to me that I have left a large hole in the middle of everything that I have had to say. This hole will always be there in any work of either criticism or of instruction. Despite analysis, praise or blame, the work in question always remains outside, a thing on its own and of its own validity. Read any of the great pieces of critical writing; they are good for themselves, they start the mind working on many things, open up new and fine tracks for it to explore, but the piece that is criticized, the thing that started it all, must remain finally aloof and on its own feet. It has its own existence, and must make its own appeal and its own recommendations to its readers, no matter what the critics may say of it. They can help it, lend it colors and values that we may not otherwise have seen, or belittle those that we might otherwise have valued, but in the end it has its own life. The same thing must be true, and in a higher degree, of any work of instruction.

Here are the recipes for making something, the suggestions of what to leave out and what to put in, the indications of fashion and change of fashion, but more than ever that hole is there. That hole is the play that will come out of all this.

I do not know that play. No one knows it, as yet. And it is that play that matters. Everything I have said is of value only if your play is the better for having heard it; and if the play is the better in spite of it, if it disregards my hints and suggestions and is a fine play of its own, that will be all right, too. There is every chance that it can be a better play. Eventually, it must be, or the theater will not be worth having. The theater moves, and its fashions change. Some of what I have written could not have been said by William Archer; the plays were not there for him to say it from. And I have gone only a very little way further. I am still in the modern realistic theater, and we are still guided by its rules, even if we have stretched them a little. We will use broader language today. We will not have to say: "They are not strangers to each other," as Aubrey Tanqueray said to Cayley Drummle when he meant that Paula and Ardale had been lovers. We will say that they were lovers. We have changed a number of our devices, broadened the scope of what we can write about, made our women honester and truer to life. We have cleared away some cant. Not all of it, by any means, and I think we must remember still that Shaw's remark was true and that the stage is twenty years behind contemporary thinking, even now, and that it is the audience, that oddly mixed audience of all kinds of taste and mentality, as well as the mere fact of its being an audience, a number of people gathered together to hear in public what it would normally regard as something for private conversation or instruction, that has helped that to stay true. But I am still bound by the conventions of the fourth wall, and the pretense that the play is really happening somewhere.

That will ultimately change, I think. We shall move forward to another kind of play. I wish I knew what it was going to be like, from which quarter the change would start to happen. Many of us hoped that expressionism was the method. It died by itself. When we first saw Thornton Wilder's plays we thought that he might have brought us the new way. He had not. He had brought only the new way for himself, as caught in his own personal, remarkable vision. There are many hopes expressed now that the verse drama, with its enrichment of the English spoken language, will be the new door. I do not think so. I have seen that door tried too often before. If I knew where the door was, I would be assaulting it myself. I still suspect that it is behind a perfectly ordinary piece of furniture, which has only to be moved, pushed aside, and there is the door that leads into the new wonderland of beauty and excitement. But I do not know which piece of furniture it is.

Perhaps you know. Perhaps the play that you are set to write is the play that will show us. In that case, this book will seem silly and old-fashioned. I shall not mind that, or if I do, then my minding will be a sign of my own retrogression into pure old-fashionedness, and will not be worth considering.

Your play will be born in you because you had something to say, and it is not unlikely that the ways that I have suggested will not fit what you had to express, and you will have found your own ways. Your play will say what to you seems beautiful and wise and important. Important, I think, not for people to have to hear, but for you, yourself, to have to say. That is what is good about it. It may seem very small to other people; to you, it will be essential. The wisdom will be your own wisdom. And the beauty—where will that come from? I think it will come, as it must come, without premeditation, perhaps even without awareness.

It is dangerous to attempt beauty, to aim for it. That determination to achieve it is apt to sound in the words you use. An English critic has recently attacked the "American playwrights who are trying to break out of the constriction of the naturalistic play-form, while at the same time retaining the realist contemporary approach." I can see his point here. The playwright is aiming at a mixture of two worlds, but his desire to leave the one is at least a good thing. The critic then goes on to deplore the lack of any "poetic approach or heightened speech." That is where I start to worry. A poetic approach, a form of heightened speech, deliberately aspired to, is apt to sound forced and a little pretentious. Beauty will not be caught that way. How is she caught? I have sometimes thought only by the author's sense of wonder, or as an actress I know has phrased it: "by the freshness of his sense of wonder." If the author can still feel a new wonder about life, and its sadness, its humor and fascination, then he will be able to communicate that wonder to the audience, and if his wonder is a keen and new and vivid thing, it will emerge as beauty. I would say that real wonder, an awareness of standing among great mysteries, is the clue to those plays which have truly moved us.

Why do we wish to express that wonder? Why do we wish to express anything at all? That is the greatest mystery of them all. Martha Graham gave a clue to it in her advice to Agnes de Mille, quoted at the end of the latter's autobiography, suggesting that there is "a life-force, an energy that is to be translated through you into action, and because there is only one of you in time, this expression is unique." The truth lies somewhere near that point. The theater may be a perishable and ephemeral commodity, but it is a powerful one, while it lasts, for conveying the author's sense of life to the world. Laughter and tears are good things. If you, as the author, have felt them for yourself, you may be able to make others feel them, too. It will take all your absorption, your deepest powers of feeling, your complete submersion in your subject matter to enable you to do so. Why you should want to, is perhaps why you were born a writer.

I spoke earlier of J. C. Squire, the poet, who gave me that earnest piece of advice that no author has ever produced a serious work of art unless he had been genuinely moved by his material. I would like to quote a quatrain of his that may make the best last word to this book. It is called "A Fresh Morning." I do not know just what he was aiming at, but he could not have aimed better had he been aiming, as I think he was, at the thing that I am trying to say. Here it is:

> Now am I a tin whistle,
> Through which God blows.
> And I wish to God I were a trumpet—
> And why, God only knows.

This book is dedicated to all who would like to be trumpets in the theater.

INDEX

INDEX